MW00620724

This Was Harrisburg

This Was

Harrisburg

A PHOTOGRAPHIC HISTORY

Richard H. Steinmetz, Sr.
and
Robert D. Hoffsommer

Foreword by Henry M. Gross

Design by Krone Art Service

Stackpole Books

THIS WAS HARRISBURG

Published by
STACKPOLE BOOKS
Cameron and Kelker Streets
P.O. Box 1831
Harrisburg, Pa. 17105

Copyright © 1976 by
Richard H. Steinmetz, Sr.
and Robert D. Hoffsommer

Printed in the U.S.A.

Library of Congress Cataloging in Publication Data

Steinmetz, Richard H
  This was Harrisburg

    1. Harrisburg, Pa.—History. I. Hoffsommer,
Robert D., joint author. II. Title.
F159.H3S76   974.8'18   75-44215
ISBN 0-8117-1729-1, Cloth
ISBN 0-8117-1983-9, Deluxe
ISBN 0-8117-2114-0, Paper

Dedicated
to the memory
of Gus M. Steinmetz,
eminent newspaper reporter, editor
and a great dad,
who ofttimes related his recollections
of happenings and personalities
pictured in this volume

-1898-

This Was Harrisburg

Photo Credits

Pictures on the following pages were taken from the collection of Warren E. Harder: 16-17 (bottom), 20, 29, 30, 32, 34, 35, 36, 42-43, 45 (top and bottom right), 47 (bottom), 48, 50, 51, 52, 53, 55 (bottom), 57, 58, 59, 60-61, 62, 63, 64, 65, 66, 69, 71, 72 (left), 73, 75 (bottom), 78, 79, 82, 83, 85, 86, 87, 88, 94, 98, 100, 101, 105, 106, 107, 108-9, 110 (bottom), 112 (bottom), 113 (bottom), 114, 118 (bottom), 119 (top), 125, 126 (top), 127, 128 (top), 129, 130, 131 (top), 132, 133, 134, 136 (top), 137, 144, 145 (bottom), 146 (bottom), 147, 148 (top), 149, 150 (bottom), 151 (bottom), 152, 153, 154, 155 (top and bottom right), 156 (top), 164 (bottom), 171 (bottom right), 173 (top and bottom), 195 (bottom), 196 (bottom), 200, 210, 211 (top), 215 (top), 216 (bottom), 217 (top and middle), and 218 (middle).

The private collection of Richard H. Steinmetz, Sr. furnished the photographs appearing on pages 21, 22, 47 (top), 49, 54, 55 (top), 68, 72 (right), 75 (top), 81, 89, 90 (bottom), 91, 92, 93, 95, 96, 97, 103, 104, 110 (top), 113 (top), 115 (top), 123 (top), 128 (bottom), 135 (bottom), 138, 139, 148 (bottom), 160 (top), 165 (top), 166, 167, 168, 169, 172, 173 (middle), 174, 175 (top), 176 (top), 177 (top), 178-79 (top), 180-81, 185, 188, 189, 190 (bottom), 191, 192 (bottom), 194 (bottom), 196-97 (top), 197 (bottom), 198, 207 (top), 209 (bottom), 216 (top and middle), and 218 (top).

Photographs on pages, 12-13, 18, 26, 37, 38-39, 67, 70, 76-77, 80, 111, 112 (top), 115 (bottom), 116, 117, 118 (top), 119 (bottom), 120, 121, 122, 123 (bottom), 124, 126 (bottom), 140-41, 145 (top), 146 (top), 150 (top), 151 (top), 156 (bottom), 157, 158-59, 160 (bottom), 161, 162, 163, 164 (top), 165 (bottom), 170 (top), 175 (bottom), 176 (bottom), 177 (bottom), 178 (bottom), 179 (bottom), 192 (top), 193, 194-95, and 199 are reproduced from the collection of William W. Stoey.

Pictures on page 90 (top), 131 (bottom), 170-71 (bottom), 171 (top), 187 (bottom), 190 (top), 201, 202-3, 204, 205, 208 (top), 211 (bottom), 212, 213, 214, 215 (middle and bottom), 217 (bottom), and 218 (bottom) come from the Pennsylvania Department of Highways photo file.

Photographs on pages 25, 44 (right), 45 (left), 102, 135 (top), and 155 (bottom left) are taken from the Hamilton family collection.

The Harrisburg YMCA furnished the photographs appearing on pages 186, 187 (top), 206, 207 (bottom), 208 (bottom), and 209 (top).

Illustrations on pages 15, 16 (top), 17 (top), and 44 (left) were provided by the Pennsylvania Historical and Museum Commission.

The photograph of James McCormick appearing on page 56 is reproduced from the rotogravure supplement of the Harrisburg Evening News dated October 5, 1935 and was furnished by the Dauphin Deposit Trust Company.

Robert Grant Crist supplied the photograph appearing on the bottom of page 136.

Foreword

Many good histories of the Harrisburg area have appeared from time to time. Pictures of Harrisburg have been available, too, but in this book, for the first time, the pictures and history are put together in a unique and interesting form.

Even those familiar with many of the subjects mentioned here will appreciate the informative captions which accompany the illustrations. As one whose family have lived in Harrisburg for five generations, my interest in historical places and people has become greater year by year, and I now recommend this book as of great value both to the historian and to persons not familiar with the history of Harrisburg.

Henry M. Gross

Preface

This Was Harrisburg relates, to a certain extent, the historical background of our city, the circumstances leading to its founding, and what has transpired during the almost 200 years since then. It does not try to be, nor can it be, all-inclusive. Rather, it emphasizes bits and pieces of everyday happenings in the lives of those who made their homes here, labored to make it a better place to live, and left a legacy that needs desperately to be perpetuated.

The story of industrial and economic growth, of civic and social development, is told with pictures rather than a wealth of printed words.

The reader will have an opportunity to view through the camera's eye, and the work of artists, the constant evolution that took place in the capital of the Keystone State from 1785 until the beginnings of World War II.

There is a good reason for limiting the coverage to that period. Developments since then have accelerated at a pace which dictates a cut-off point.

The intent of the authors is to impress upon the younger generations how fast and how far we have come in a very short period of history.

The reader will have an opportunity to peer into the past. He will see other generations of residents at work and at play, in happy and unhappy circumstances, together with the results of their labors in a material and spiritual sense.

This we present with no apologies for sins of commission or omission, which undoubtedly exist.

Acknowledgments

Had it not been for the enthusiasm of a real estate salesman, the late Warren Harder, in the hobby of collecting old-time photographs of Harrisburg, and a passion for recording on film day-to-day life in the city during the late 1890s and early 1900s by a professional taxidermist and a darned good amateur photographer, William W. Stoey, this book would have been a rather ordinary collection of period photographs.

But William Stoey's intuition for accentuating the then normal things of life, and Warren Harder's deep-seated desire to preserve them, has brought into reality a pictorial history of the capital city of Pennsylvania that is both unusual and informative.

Fortunately both the Stoey and Harder collections have been preserved and safely stored in the Archives of our Commonwealth. Here they are watched over by a very pleasant and helpful curator, Mrs. Dana Beyers, whose patience and knowledge brought to light a host of old-time pictures, many of which have never previously been exposed to public view.

In addition to Mrs. Beyers, the many courtesies extended by other members of the Archives staff are greatly appreciated.

Likewise was the assistance so ably given by Mrs. Becky Lawhead, a substitute teacher in the East Pennsboro Township School District, and Robert Grant Crist, local historian, who furnished Civil War photos and considerable good advice.

More help came from Mrs. John Tillman, curator for the Dauphin County Historical Society, who permitted unlimited use of the library and photo collection owned by the society and preserved in the old Harris Mansion. Thanks also go to Charles Pugh, chairman of the Capitol Area Transportation Authority, who kindly provided much needed information regarding local transportation, and Benjamin S. Peters, Jr., of Camp Hill.

Local newspaper files, previous historical publications, and verbal answers to questions all combined to make possible reasonably accurate captions for the nearly three hundred pictures that comprise the bulk of this book.

Again, the authors wish to extend their heartfelt thanks to all who did their part in the creation of a pictorial history of Harrisburg.

The father of the founder of Harrisburg was reputed to have been the victim of an attempted burning at the stake by a passing war party. This diorama depicts the event, which culminated in a rescue by friendly Indians camped nearby.

Chapter 1

In the Beginning...

In the beginning there were the mountains and the forests, the river and the valley. Looking down, circling hawks and bald eagles saw a vast, undulating carpet of green, broken only by the bright, wavering ribbon of the river as it surged through the gaps in successive Blue Ridge Mountain ridges to flow in mile-wide majesty past the future site of Harrisburg.

From their vantage point in the air the birds could also see—gray above the green of the forest—the smoke of Indian campfires, usually where smaller streams emptied into the river. In the years before the coming of the white man, the valley of the Susquehanna was truly the red man's happy hunting ground. Here was a moderate climate with not-too-cold winters, fertile soil for the growing of corn, beans, squash, and tobacco, abundant wildlife, and the river for food fish. More important, the river furnished a broad highway for travel.

Those expert in these matters have estimated that the Indian population of Pennsylvania 250 years ago scarcely exceeded 20,000. This would come to an average of about one red man to every two and a quarter square miles. If this be correct, then it must be equally true that 1000 to 1500, or perhaps even more of those 20,000, lived in that part of the Susquehanna Valley adjoining present-day Harrisburg. Archaeologists are still discovering the sites of Indian villages which were once relatively permanent.

The term "relatively permanent" is used advisedly. Most of those Indians were essentially homebodies. Although in times of war or famine, or even on social occasions, a whole village might move at an hour's notice, this does not appear to have been the case with the Susquehanna Valley's early Indians. Their palisaded villages were built for permanence.

What was the life of those long-ago dwellers along the river? What were they called? The earliest records, at the beginning of the seventeenth century, name them as Susquehannocks. However, archaeological research indicates that some time before that, a tribe of the Algonquian group once occupied the Valley. The latter group included the Delaware and the Shawnee, who apparently had moved in from the south and east.

The name "Susquehannock" obviously derived from the Indian name for the river; appropriately, Susquehanna is translated as "the stream that falls toward the south." Another less poetic interpretation is "long-crooked-river."

It is known from the accounts left by the earliest white men in the Harrisburg area that the Susquehannocks lived in villages made up of communal houses of varying lengths up to 100 feet. Five or more families lived in each house, the family groups being separated by partitions, usually of bark. Each family did its own cooking and had its own chimney hole in the roof. In short, the Susquehannocks were apparently among the first Americans to live in apartment houses.

The redoubtable Captain John Smith of Jamestown Colony fame was very possibly the first European to meet men of the Susquehannock tribe. In 1608 he led an expedition exploring up Chesapeake Bay and some distance up the river to about where Deposit, Maryland is today. Here he met some fifty or sixty Susquehannock warriors from villages at or near the site of present-day Harrisburg. They came at his request, he reported; it could quite as likely have been curiosity that brought them when word of his approach reached the villages.

Smith was strongly impressed by the size, dress, and dignified bearing of the red men. His comment is worth quoting at length:

Upon this river inhabit a people called Susquesahanock. They are seated 2 daies higher than was passage for the discoverers Barge. . . . 60 of those Susquesahanocks came to the discoverers with skins, Bowes, Arrows, Targets, Beads, Swords, and Tobacco pipes for presents. Such great and well proportioned men, are seldom seen, for they seemed like giants to the English, yea and to the neighbors; yet seemed to be of an honest and simple disposition (and they were) with much adoe restrained from adoring the discoverers as Gods. Those are the most strange people of all those Countries, both in language and attire; for their language it may well beseeme their proportions, sounding from them, as it were a great voice in a vault, or cave, as an Eccho. Their

Typical Susquehannock Indian village that existed in the area of present-day Harrisburg when John Harris explored the frontier in search of trade with the Indians.

attire is the skinnes of Beares and Woolves, and some have cassacks made of Beares heades and skinnes that a mans necke goes through the skinnes necke, and the eares of the beare fastened to his shoulders behind, and the nose and the teeth hanging down his breast, and at the end of the nose hung a Beares Pawe; the half sleeves comming to the elbowes were neckes of Beares and the armes through the mouth, with pawes hanging at their noses. One had the head of a woolfe hanging in a chain for a Jewell; his tobacco pipe 3 quarters of a yard long, prettily carved with a Bird, a Beare, a deare, or some such devise at the great end, sufficient to beat out the braines of a man; with bowes, arrowes, and clubs, suitable to their greatness and conditions . . . .

Smith goes on to describe the largest of the Susquehannocks:

The calfe of . . . leg was 3 quarters of a yard about; and all the rest of his limbs so answerable to that proportion, that he seemed the goodliest man that ever we beheld. His haire, the one side was long, and the other shore close with a ridge over his crown like a cocks combe. His arrowes were 5 quarters (of a yard) long, headed with flints or splinters of stones, in form like a heart, an inch broad, and an inch and a halfe or more long. These hee wore in a woolves skinne at his backe for his quiver, his bow in the one hand and his clubbe in the other . . . .

Smith knew the Virginia Indians; it must be assumed that he regarded the Susquehanna red men as their superiors. Certainly later white men spoke admiringly of the Susquehannocks in comparison with other tribes.

Incidentally, Smith's voyage of exploration almost ended disastrously. On the return trip down Chesapeake Bay the party amused themselves by spearing fish with their swords. Smith impaled an odd-looking creature which stung him on the arm with its tail as he removed it from his sword. In a few minutes he was suffering such intense pain that all expected him to die; they even dug a grave for him on a nearby island. He recovered, however—enough to eat the fish that had stung him!—and commemorated the event by giving the island a name, Stingray Isle.

Life in the palisaded Susquehannock villages followed the usual Indian pattern: the women took full charge of their garden plots, planting, cultivating, and harvesting the crops, preparing meals, making clothing, and performing the other numerous domestic tasks. It may be noted that it was they who, combining green corn and beans, made the happy gastronomic marriage which they called *msiguatash*, later gratefully named by the white men—succotash. The men hunted and fished, and participated in war and hunting parties. They were a comparatively peaceful tribe, powerful enough to discourage attack, and lacking the usual incentives of plunder and glory that motivated other less fortunately located tribes.

It was a matriarchal society, the clans in the tribe taking their names from the distaff side. The children led happier

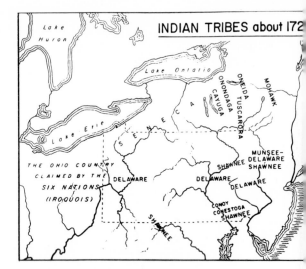

From the records of early explorers and later archaeologists the locations of the various Indian tribes in Pennsylvania and neighboring New York were established as indicated on the accompanying map.

Penn's Woods was criss-crossed with Indian trails. The locations of these paths when Harris and other traders were doing business with the natives have been established from early communications with government officials and from early maps.

An early painting depicting the Harris trading post on the east bank of the Susquehanna close to the present site of the Harris Mansion, now headquarters of the Dauphin County Historical Society. It has been determined that John Harris, Sr. had been trading with the Indians in this area before he established his home here in 1728.

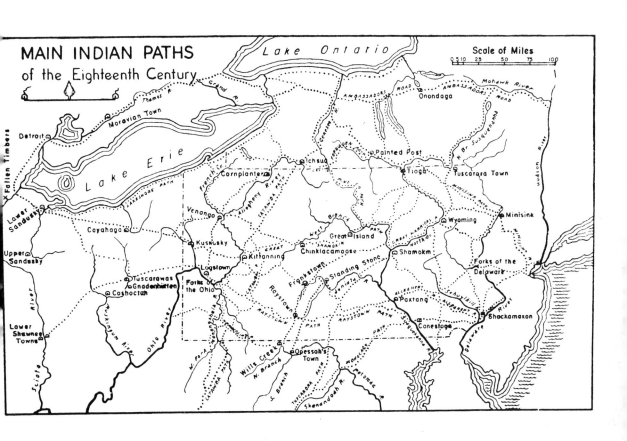

The Kelso Ferry House was one of the first buildings erected on the West Shore opposite Harris Ferry. John Harris built it in 1734 and it was leased by him to William Kelso, who assisted in the operation of Harris Ferry. In later years it stood in the shadow of the Cumberland Valley Railroad Bridge until the early 1900s, when it was torn down.

lives than many modern youngsters, playing, helping their mothers in small household duties, and receiving instruction from their fathers in the serious business of survival in the wilderness.

The Susquehannocks were a branch of the powerful Iroquoian group, whose tribes were scattered all the way along the course of the Susquehanna from its headwaters in western New York to Chesapeake Bay. They were known by other names. The early Swedes and Dutch called them Minquas and the French labeled them Andaste. The latter is a corruption of the name Conestoga given the Indians by early settlers in Pennsylvania. The tribe came to be known as Conestogas; it was under that name that the "Paxton Boys" wiped out the pitiful last remnants of the tribe in the vicious massacre of 1763.

In 1615 the Susquehannocks were probably at the height of their power, wealth, and influence. It was in the autumn of that year that the first white man passed through the length of the Susquehanna River basin. He was Estienne Brule, interpreter for the great French explorer Samuel de Champlain, founder of Quebec, who gave his name to New York's largest lake. Brule spent the autumn and winter among the Indians as he traversed the river down to Chesapeake Bay. His report, as given by Champlain, provides us with our first "official" knowledge of the Susquehanna Valley Indians and their way of life. He, like Captain John Smith, was much impressed.

About this same time the Dutch and the Swedes began to move in from the Delaware, lured by the prospect of wealth from trade with the Susquehannocks in furs, largely beaver and otter. In those far-off days the river valley and the tributary streams, mainly the Juniata and the West Branch to the north, swarmed with beaver, otter, muskrats, deer, foxes, and other fur bearers. And beaver skins were in tremendous demand then in Europe and even as far away as China. This trade, particularly with the Dutch, had actually begun before Estienne Brule made his historic voyage down the river, but in the years following that trip the commerce in furs swelled from a trickle to a torrent as the Indians traded skins for hatchets, knives, guns, powder, lead—and rum. Contact now was easier as the Dutch and Swedes pushed westward, building forts to protect their trading posts along the lines of age-old Indian trails.

These trails and the river—itself a broad, smooth, easy path for traffic— account for the manner in which the white man moved westward in the settlement of Pennsylvania. Men soon learned that the overland trails of the Indians were unsurpassed from the standpoints of natural surveying and engineering. They took advantage of "the lay of the land" for the easiest travel, along ridges or the high ground of the river banks.

More particularly, it was the trails that finally determined the location of Harrisburg. At this point, where Yorkshire-born John Harris came to establish his ferry and trading post, the great Iroquois war trail crossed the Susquehanna to traverse the Cumberland Valley, cross the Potomac, and wind down through Virginia into the Carolinas. It was a two-way trail, for just as the Iroquois used it to raid the Catawbas of South Carolina, so warriors of that tribe made the long journey northward to revenge themselves upon the Iroquois of the Susquehanna Valley. The Scotch-Irish settlers in and about present Paxtang suffered from their proximity to this war trail.

There was also an east-west trail that ran eventually into the Ohio Valley to the west, and to Philadelphia and the Delaware to the east. This was largely a trade trail for the Indians coming east with their bundles of furs for barter with the white man, and for the more ventursome traders going into the "backwoods," as the wilderness beyond the Susquehanna Valley was called. And of course—and finally—there was the river, the trail along which one red man in a canoe could transport more furs more easily than could three or four Indians on land. These were the main trails; like branches of a tree, minor paths fed into them to swell the constant traffic that passed the site of future Harrisburg.

Oddly—and unfortunately—we have no authenticated record of events in the

Susquehanna Valley for almost 100 years from Estienne Brule's historic visit in 1615 to the time when Colonial Lieutenant Governor John Evans headed a posse to Paxtang in 1707 to apprehend Nicole Godin, a trader who had been illegally selling rum to the Indians, and about whom much complaint must have been made to have reached the authorities and caused the Council to take action. It is known that about 1675 the northerly Iroquois subjugated the Susquehannocks, so reducing them that they could not resist a gradual influx of Delawares, or Lenape, from the east along the Delaware River, and of Shawnees from the Carolinas.

In a sense, the visit of Lieutenant Governor Evans set the stage—historically—for the coming of John Harris. Here again the time of his arrival cannot be pinpointed at the place his name was to make famous. It may have been around 1725, for in 1727 there is an entry in the Proprietor of Pennsylvania's Minute Books of the Board of Property:

"John Harris requests (by John Warder) 500 acres of land above Pextang, on Susquahanna River." Since energetic Scotch-Irish about that time had begun to make claims on the fertile lands in Paxtang and the surrounding area, it seems reasonable to assume that an alert business man such as John Harris would lose little time in putting in his bid. He had proved his business ability earlier in Philadelphia and at his trading post at Conoy (now Bainbridge, Lancaster County).

Coincidentally, the year 1727 marked the beginning of the mass migration of the resident Shawnee and Delaware tribes from the Susquehannocks' former lands, the Shawnees westward to the Ohio Valley, and the Delawares both north to the upper Susquehanna and west to Ohio. The leader of the Shawnee movement was the half-breed Shawnee chief, Peter Chartier, famous in the early history of Harrisburg's neighbor across the river, New Cumberland. So rapidly did the migration take place that

In the year 1785 the son of the first settler on the site of Harrisburg hired William Maclay to lay out a plot plan for a town which he hoped would become the capital of his native state. His hopes were realized a few years later. Shown here is a reproduction of the original plot plan for the town at Harris Ferry, which after some dispute has borne the family name ever since.

Early stone buildings mingle with more modern brick structures in Hummelstown's square today as they did back in 1925 when the accompanying photo was taken. A trolley from Harrisburg had just met another from Hershey and the crews are socializing before boarding their cars for the return trip. Note the curbside gasoline pumps. "Antique" cars, by modern standards, are parked indiscriminately without causing any traffic problems.

by the following year most of the Shawnees and Delawares had decamped, leaving empty villages behind.

So John Harris came to Paxtang—not the place of the present borough to the east of modern Harrisburg, but to a small Indian village, Pextang, located near where Paxtang Creek flows into the Susquehanna. As a canny trader he recognized the commercial value of this crossroads of Indian trails. Here he built his trading post—a house and several sheds—and applied himself to the establishment of friendly relations with the Indians. He later planned to expand his operations by building a second trading post at the mouth of the Juniata, but objections by the Indians caused him to abandon the project.

Nevertheless he prospered; in the Colonial Records for 1734 we find this note:

John Harris of Pextan having in Xber last obtained the Proprs. Grant for the sole keeping of the Ferry over Susquahanna River at Pextan, hath now applied to the Prop'r for Liberty

to Build a small house on the west side of the said River for the Conveniency of Travellers that may happen to come on that side in the Night Season or in Stormy Weather when the Boat or Flat cannot pass. He also requests the grant of 200 acres of Land on the same side of the River opposite to his Plantation where he dwells and whereon he would build the House.

The Proprietor, Thomas Penn, granted the request for the "small house," stipulating in the Penn tradition "provided the Indians be not made uneasy by it," but withheld for a time the land grant.

The record thus fixes 1733 as the year when Harris' ferry began operation, transporting men and goods across the river. As nearly as any date, 1733 also marks the real beginning of the westward surge of the white man's civilization and the consequent slow retreat of the red man before it. In the clash of the two ways of life, the superiority of the

The sylvan beauty of what was Paxtang Park testifies to its attraction for the early settlers. Located in a little valley that once served as a gateway to John Harris' ferry, it was a popular picnic spot for Harrisburg families for many years. The "Indian Spring" over which Thomas Rutherford built his springhouse provided water for an artificial lake and a meandering stream that still flows towards the wide Susquehanna.

First company in the United States to manufacture steel in marketable quantities, the Pennsylvania Steel Company built its plant and established a town adjacent to Harrisburg in 1866. The company prospered as did the community and the entire area. In the early 1900s, when this view was circulated in postcard form, the plant had expanded to approximately its present size. In 1916 the Steelton plant was taken over by the Bethlehem Steel Company. It still provides employment for many Harrisburgers.

white man in weapons and numbers, his persistence, and his thirst for land and wealth made the result inevitable—and sadly so. For if the white man conquered in the end, he also lost something. Though the red man had his faults—and they were many and serious—he had virtues that might well be emulated today. And to the shame of the white man he has treated conquered foreign enemies far more generously than he has dealt with the Indians whose lands he preempted.

It was a new chapter in the history of Pennsylvania, this westward push of settlers and traders. For a time John Harris' trading post was a focal point for traffic, with trails converging there like the spokes in a wheel to the hub. When overtrapping and the consequent scarcity of beaver and otter resulted from the demand for their fur, the market shifted to deerskins, the "buckskins" of colonial times, commonly called "bucks." They became the standard of value in frontier trade, which perhaps explains the modern term we use colloquially for a dollar.

Up to his death in December, 1748, John Harris had a genuinely friendly interest in the Indians, a friendliness that went beyond the self-serving, artificial friendship of the average trader. His son, the second John Harris, founder of Harrisburg, continued this tradition. His trading house became a great visiting place for Indians from the north, south, and west, and during his lifetime the younger Harris met chiefs from as far west as the Ohio Valley, as far north as western New York, and from the south the chiefs of the Delaware tribes migrating up into the former lands of the Susquehannocks. The names of some of the chiefs are worth remembering, for the friendship or enmity they bore the English affected the outcome of the great struggle of the French and the English for dominance in the New World—the contest known as the French and Indian War.

One of these chiefs was Scarouady (or

Monacatootha), an Oneida chieftain in the great Iroquois Confederation. An early friend of the English and a frequent visitor in Harris' home, he served as a guide in Braddock's ill-fated expedition against the French at Fort Duquesne. Another was Peter Chartier, the half-breed Shawnee chief mentioned earlier. Though he was often at Harris' post, living as he did for a time just across the river at present New Cumberland, after he took his Shawnees west to the Ohio he threw in his lot with the French.

A third chief was Shikellamy; his is the best-known name to Harrisburgers, many of whom fondly remember happy days as boys at the YMCA's Camp Shikellimy. He also was an Oneida Iroquois; from his village of Shamokin (present-day Sunbury) he paid many visits to Harris, with whom, in spite of occasional minor disagreements, he was a close friend. A fourth chief, Sassoonan, head chief of the Delawares, lived for a time at Paxtang before moving upriver to Shamokin; he too valued Harris as a friend.

Another visitor to Harris Ferry was the colorful Chief Sattelihu, known better, perhaps, as Andrew Montour. He too lived across the river from Harris, on Conodoguinet Creek. The story of his varied adventures as guide, interpreter, and fighter for the English could be made into an exciting romantic novel. He knew Conrad Weiser and Count Zinzendorf; the latter's description of him in 1742 is interesting in that it shows the dress of the Indian chiefs of that time, in contrast to the popular concept of the half-naked savage:

He wore a brown broadcloth coat, a scarlet damasken lappel-waistcoat, breeches, over which his shirt hung, a black Cordovan neckerchief, decked with silver bugles, shoes and stockings, and a hat. His ears were hung with pendants of brass and other wires plaited together like the handle of a basket . . . .

Another of Harris' chieftain friends was Tanachharison, half-king of the Iroquois. It would be hard to overrate the value of his loyalty to the English in the troubled times along the frontier in the conflict with the French. And he was perhaps the younger Harris' closest Indian friend. He died at Harris' home in 1754, and Scarouady, inheritor of the half-kingship, told Harris: "Keep him with you, because he is one with you in heart, and we trust his body with you, because he loved your people."

So, for almost two and a quarter centuries the bones of that loyal friend have lain in an unknown grave beside the Susquehanna, somewhere near the last resting place of the first John Harris. One likes to fancy that his brooding spirit still lingers protectively over the bustling city that now covers the wilderness he once roamed and loved.

It is not the purpose of this book to present a detailed, exhaustive—and probably exhausting—history of Harrisburg and Dauphin County. But a few more facts and dates are necessary to set the stage for this picture-story of the city. And no book on Harrisburg could be called complete without the story of the first John Harris and the mulberry tree. There is no recorded and authenticated basis for the story, only family tradition, but tradition so strong that many researchers of the city's history are inclined to accept it. And it does make a good story.

Sometime in the early years, after Harris had established his trading post, a band of Iroquois returning after a raid to the south stopped at Harris' home to demand rum. Since they were already rather drunk from liquor sold to them as they came up the Cumberland Valley, Harris very properly refused. The angered Indians seized him, dragged him out and tied him to a mulberry tree near the river bank, then proceeded to gather wood for a "burning at the stake." Before the fire was lighted, a band of friendly Shawnees from across the river, summoned by Harris' devoted slave Hercules, arrived by canoe in the traditional "nick of time" to save the father of the city's founder. In gratitude, Harris promptly freed Hercules. Those who enjoy considering coincidences and consequences might interestingly maintain the probability that Harrisburg owes its existence to the faithful devotion of a black slave, for the chances are that the drink-crazed savages would not have spared the Harris family.

So impressed was Harris by his deliverance that he insisted on being buried under that same mulberry. The family had wished to bury him in the old Paxton Church graveyard; if they did that, he vowed, he would rise from the grave and walk back to the mulberry tree. So he had his way. One may go today and read the inscription on the stone that marks his grave under a descendant of that mulberry tree, along the riverbank not far from the sturdy stone house his son built:

A CRUCE SALUS
John Harris
Of Yorkshire England
The Friend Of
WILLIAM PENN
And Father Of The
Founder of Harrisburg
Died Dec. 17, 1748
In the Communion of The
Church of England

John Harris II, even more enterprising than his father, now took over the business. Though he consolidated his relations with the Indians and though Harris Ferry was made an important depot for military and other supplies, the settlement around the ferry grew very slowly in the years immediately following the death of the first Harris. In 1756 a report to the Governor and Council, then seeking a place of meeting for a treaty with the Indians, stated " . . . as at Harris' there was but one single House and few Conveniences, Mr. Weiser was called in and asked if it might not be better to hold it at Carlisle . . . ."

Six years earlier (January 27, 1750) Cumberland County had been officially established. It embraced the present area of Dauphin County. Carlisle was the county seat.

Though the settlement was not growing, Harris' business continued to prosper. In 1763 he secured from Governor James Hamilton a two-year license to continue his ferry at a yearly fee of ten silver shillings, with assurance that no other ferry would be permitted for a mile and a quarter above and below on the river.

The close of the seven-year French and Indian War in 1763 swelled the stream of emigration westward, and Harris Ferry stood in the path of that stream. John Harris soon saw opportunities. When Dauphin County was established in 1785, Harris had already proposed (1784) to the Assembly the laying out of a town of 200 quarter-acre lots on the higher ground upriver from his house. As a result, Harris Ferry was made the county seat.

So, in the spring of 1785, William Maclay—Harris' son-in-law and later first United States senator from Pennsylvania—laid out the town which he named Harrisburg, arranging lots to provide for a courthouse, jail, and public square, and alloting a square of four acres to the State of Pennsylvania "for such purposes as the Government may apply the same . . . ." Either Harris with remarkable prescience saw his town as Pennsylvania's capital, or he was superlatively optimistic about the future of a community which then consisted of only one house—his own.

A quotation from the journal of Theophile Cazenove, a Frenchman traveling in Pennsylvania in 1794, indicates the result of Harris' foresight:

The old stone house built over a never-failing spring by Thomas and Jean Rutherford in 1755 still stands in Paxtang, on the south side of the Reading Railroad tracks. It is another one of Harrisburg's historic landmarks and is close to a recently established bypass between Derry and Paxton streets, which follows the route of a pioneer packhorse trail.

This city is one of America's little phenomena, in the matter of rapidity of its rise. In 1785 there was on this location only the single house and farm of Mr. Harris. The favorable situation of the place gave him the idea of founding a city there; he laid out the streets on a wise plan, like the city of Philadelphia, but keeping a large square in the center . . . . There are about a thousand lots and already 300 houses neatly built in brick or "logs and mortar," 2 stories high, English windows; the streets are wide, not yet paved . . . 32 taverns and eighteen merchants keeping in their stores European merchandise and buying farmers' produce . . . .

Thus Harrisburg had become a settled town of permanent homes in ten years. Dauphin County (early called Dauphine) had a population not quite equal to long-established Cumberland County. But city and county had begun the growth that would continue to the present day.

Friendship with France was at its peak in the years immediately following the Revolutionary War. Dauphin County, named after the Dauphine of France, was one result; in 1786 came another, officially changing "Harrisburg" to "Louisburg." However, five years later the Assembly made the town a borough and restored the original name (in April 1791). So, before he died, John Harris II had the satisfaction of knowing that his name would be perpetuated in the town that he had founded.

Said to be almost as old as the town itself, the hotel at Dauphin still serves the public today. When the above picture was taken in the 1890s, David Hoffman was the genial proprietor, according to James Megonnell, Sr., Dauphin R.D. The old inn has had a number of owners since then, the present being Mr. Megonnell's nephew, Richard H. Megonnell.

Chapter 2

Harris and Harrisburg's Neighbors

On April 14, 1785, five commissioners of the newly established Dauphin County reported favorably to the State Assembly on John Harris II's proposal to donate land which he would lay out for a town. Exactly a century later, April 14, 1885, A. Boyd Hamilton, Sr., himself a memorable figure in the history of Harrisburg, addressed the Dauphin County Historical Society as a part of Harrisburg's and Dauphin County's centennial celebration. In his speech he gave a description of the founder of our city. It is worth quoting, for it gives the human touch to one who otherwise remains only a shadowy figure:

I have conversed with many persons who knew Mr. Harris before 1785, and from that date to the period of his death in 1791, had much social and business intercourse with him. He is described as a tall, well proportioned sturdy man, with good teeth, smooth shaven, healthy appearance, and hair inclined to turn gray from an original rich brown. This he wore in the fashion of his time, long, and upon the Fourth of July had it powdered. His dress was "leather breeches," in the fit of which he took great pride; brown coat and vest, long white woolen stockings, silver buckles and heavy low-cut shoes;

fond of his gun, rod and dog; and equally fond of fishing or of a shooting-match; quite an adept at "long bullets," or shuffle-board. He did not hesitate about expressing an opinion upon any subject of discussion, and was most emphatic in his admiration of Washington and those who had served under him. He lived long enough to see his town well started on the way to its present proportions.

A history of Harrisburg, no matter how brief, ought to be supplemented by mention at least of some of its neighboring communities. To discuss them all, however, would too much enlarge this book to a history of Dauphin and its adjoining counties. Ten nearby communities—a good round number—have nevertheless been arbitrarily chosen for brief comment. Each could have—and some do have—extensive written histories of their own.

STEELTON

Next door to Harrisburg on the south along the river, Steelton—at one time second in population to the capital—got its start in 1866 when the Pennsylvania Steel Company erected its plant there. It was the first in the United States operating solely to make steel, and was first also in the manufacture of steel rails. Most of the ore used came from the famous Cornwall ore bank near Lebanon. The first post office (1871) took the name Steel Works, but in 1880 this was changed to Steelton, the name subsequently adopted when the town was incorporated. The company was later (1916) taken over by the Bethlehem Steel Company. Steelton not only produces fine steel; it also turns out fine athletes. The community is known for fielding excellent teams in all sports, with little Steelton High School a powerful rival first of old Central and Tech, later of John Harris and William Penn, and more recently of the now consolidated Harrisburg High School.

PAXTANG

Now a borough, Paxtang was prominent in the early history of this area. It was here that some of the first of the sturdy Scotch-Irish settlers located, built the log church that was the forerunner of historic Paxton Presbyterian Church, and began to cultivate the land. Since so much of Paxtang's history relates to that church and to Harrisburg, it will be dealt with more fully in chapter 3.

Perhaps here is as good a place as any to clear up the confusion between the names Paxton and Paxtang. Today the name of both the creek and the Presbyterian church is Paxton. This discrepancy between the name of the borough and the name of the creek and church arises from the fact that as the white settlers changed their pronunciation of the Indian name, they changed its spelling, and this lack of uniformity has persisted to the present day.

Originally Paxtang was an isolated village, separated from Harrisburg by open fields and patches of woodland; now the growth of both communities makes it difficult for the casual visitor to tell where one begins and the other ends. Back in the early decades of the present

century, the Harrisburg Railways Company developed an amusement park—appropriately Paxtang Park—on the southern outskirts of the village. Electric trolley cars—open-sided ones in the summer—ran to the park, which in its heyday boasted a little zoo, a theater, a small lake for boating—where also one summer three elephants of a vaudeville act took their daily baths—a swimming pool, a tennis court, a carousel (merry-go-round), and the usual refreshment and amusement stands and souvenir booths.

But like so many pleasant things of the past, these are now "gone with the wind." Even those who as children knew the park well can now scarcely identify the landscape, changed as it is by roads, highway overpass, and apartment houses. Only the old stone house of Thomas Rutherford, built over a spring in 1755 and reputedly the oldest dwelling in central Pennsylvania, remains near the entrance to the park. But the spring, whose stream once fed the lake, still gushes up from between the foundation walls to flow past what was once known as the County Poor Farm on one side and the county "pest house" (a small frame building on a hillside above the creek, used for isolation treatment of smallpox cases) on the other, on its leisurely way to the Susquehanna.

MIDDLETOWN

This community has the distinction of being the oldest town in Dauphin County; it dates back to 1761. It was so named from its position halfway between the larger settlements of Lancaster and Carlisle. Located near the point where Swatara Creek flows into the Susquehanna, it was once one of the principal markets for the timber that came down the river in great rafts, particularly in the spring. In fact, most of the merchandise of the town once came by water, loaded on "keel boats," flat-bottom, shallow-draft boats fifty or more feet long, capable of carrying a considerable tonnage in cargo. Though rafting and keel boating stopped long ago, the town—third largest in the county—has continued to flourish. Undisturbed by too much "progress," Middletown is still full of old houses to delight students of early Pennsylvania architecture.

HUMMELSTOWN

The plotting of this town was done in 1762 by Frederick Hummel. It bore the name Frederickstown until after Hum-

many old names still survive in the town. A Harrisburg Railways trolley line once connected Hummelstown with Harrisburg; now excellent highways serve the town and adjoining communities.

HIGHSPIRE

Located along the line of the Pennsylvania Railroad about six miles from Harrisburg, the community was designated a post town even prior to 1812. It went through an in-and-out existence as a borough; it was incorporated in 1867, but the Legislature annulled the charter

The village of Highspire was not only noted for making whiskey, it also boasted a canalboat yard during the heyday of the state's public works program. Boatbuilding was a profitable business for many years, and William Frick provided the local economy a boost by the use of local labor. The photo was taken in the 1870s.

mel's death, when it was changed to take his last name. It is probably the only town in the United States to have carried at separate times the Christian name and the surname of its founder. Its settlement was slow, since during the Revolutionary War most of the men of the vicinity were serving with the Continental Army. Several gunsmiths lived in the town at that time, making and repairing weapons for the Army. At the end of the war the population, except for a few Scotch-Irish, was chiefly German, and

the next year. It then again was incorporated as a borough in 1904. In its early history the borough's name was famous for a rye whiskey made by the Highspire Distillery and later by the Highspire Distilling Company. The Eighteenth Amendment modified the borough's industry, but it is still a growing community.

Archaeologists have found artifacts indicating that the borough is built on the site of a prehistoric Susquehannock Indian village.

HERSHEY

Advertised as "Chocolatetown, U.S.A.," Hershey is unique as the youngest town among Harrisburg's neighbors. Laid out by Milton Snavely Hershey in 1903, it is one of the showplaces of Pennsylvania, not merely for the modern plant where candy and dozens of chocolate and cocoa products are manufactured for shipment all over the world, but for its splendid hotel, sports stadium, convention center, theater, amusement park, and zoo. And Founder's Hall, beautifully set in the rolling countryside south of the town, is a memorable place to visit.

Hershey is most deservedly famous for the system of homes and education provided by the founder for orphaned boys. It is a "company town" in the best sense. Here, not far from the busy center of town, is the original Old Derry Presbyterian Church, built in 1732 and now preserved in a glass-walled house for protection against the weather.

ROCKVILLE

About five miles up the river from Harrisburg is Rockville, originally called Bushy Rock. The town, laid out by Mrs. Matilda Cox in 1834 (though first settled in 1774), offers at least three notable attractions to the visitor: the beautiful view from the mountain above of the majestic sweep of the river and the grandeur of the mountain ranges; the longest stone-arch bridge in the world; and nearby, the site of historic Fort Hunter, built in 1755-56. The latter was one of the frontier forts erected along the upper Susquehanna to protect

Hoover's Canal Hotel at Rockville was in its twilight years in 1890, when this photograph was taken. Morgan Hoover, the proprietor, and his family together with hired help pose on the front steps of the inn, which stood for many years afterwards, only to be ravaged by the Flood of 1936.

against the French-inspired Indian raids not uncommon at the start of the French and Indian War.

DAUPHIN

Three miles farther up the river lies the little community of Dauphin. Once it was expected that it would be a bustling center of transportation and industry. For various reasons these hopes never materialized, for which today's residents are probably grateful. Innis Green laid out the town in 1826 and named it Port Lyon. Shortly thereafter townspeople renamed it Greensburg to honor the founder. At incorporation as a borough in 1845 it took the name Dauphin, but was later sometimes referred to as Port Dauphin. In its palmy days the Pennsylvania Canal traffic made it a busy place, but with the decline of water transport and the growth of railroads and then highway transport, the town reverted to a slower pace and became a pleasant community of permanent and summer residents.

HALIFAX

The borough lies about nine miles farther up the Susquehanna near the mouth of Armstrong's Creek, the latter named after the earliest settler. In 1756 Fort Halifax, named for Lord Halifax, was built at the mouth of the creek (an old map shows it some distance from the creek) to serve as a munitions magazine to reinforce Fort Augusta at Shamokin (Sunbury) to the north and Harris Ferry to the south during the frontier wars.

The renegade Simon Girty lived here or nearby for a time. "Girty's Notch" on the river's western shore perpetuates his infamous name. The town was laid out in 1784 by George Sheaffer and Peter Rise. Strange as it seems now, one of the town's earliest industries was its very profitable shad fisheries in the spring. Halifax became a borough in 1875.

ESTHERTOWN

Originally Estherton and later Coxestown, the community will not be found on modern maps. One of the oldest towns in Dauphin County, it was absorbed in the northward spread of Harrisburg. Laid out along the river a short distance below the later Jonestown Road by Dr. John Cox, Jr. during the French and Indian War, and named after his wife, it was a supply depot during Sullivan's expedition in 1779. It is interesting to note that on the William Scull map of "Improvements in Pennsylvania" (1770) the towns of Esther Town, Hummels Town, and Middle Town are named with the capital letters used for large, important towns; Pextang (*sic*) with the large, lower-case letters for minor communities; and Harris's (*sic*) Ferry with *very* small italics.

The ten communities briefly covered have one thing in common: they are all less than twenty miles from Harrisburg, most of them much less, and for that reason they have to some small degree been influenced by, or have influenced the development of Harrisburg. To take an obvious example: what would Paxtang have been but for Harrisburg, and how would Harrisburg have developed had there been no Paxtang?

Still, despite the fact that the trade and industry of these various adjoining communities were beneficial to Harrisburg's growth, such influence was at best but indirect or supplementary. Of more importance was the fact that Harrisburg's riverside location—at the hub of converging Indian trails and the later canals, railroads, and highways that were built over them—ideally suited the city for growth and a prosperous future.

When pioneers of the Scotch-Presbyterian faith moved into this area they built a log church at Paxtang. By 1740 their number had increased and the sanctuary of the present stone structure, pictured in this recent photograph, was built. It was the first church to serve residents of Harris Ferry and vicinity.

Chapter 3

The First Churches

The early settlers of the Harrisburg community took their religion seriously. That was, after all, why they chose to come to Pennsylvania, with its unique promise of absolute freedom of worship.

In telling the history of the city one cannot lightly pass over its early churches; they colored the thinking and influenced the actions of its first citizens to an incalculable extent.

The first Scotch-Irish Presbyterians came to Paxtang on the Susquehanna and then spread east along the shallow creek valley to the area of present-day Paxtang and beyond. Almost simultaneously with the building of their homes, they put up their log church. Here, according to generations-old tradition, preaching began in 1716. The first regular preacher, however, came ten years later—the Reverend James Anderson of Donegal.

The official organization into a Presbyterian church (what is now Paxton Presbyterian Church) took place in 1732 by action of the Presbytery of Donegal. Eight years later, in 1740, the log meetinghouse was replaced by the present stone building, which now has the distinction of being the oldest Presbyterian church building in continuous use in Pennsylvania, and the second oldest in the United States. According to his great-grandson, John Harris furnished the stone for its construction. The interior underwent four successive remodelings from 1847 to 1888 before being restored to its original appearance in 1931.

For more than thirty-five years it was the only regular place of worship in the slowly growing community. Tradition has it that during that time a log schoolhouse, at what is now Third and Walnut streets, was used for worship on the infrequent occasions when a minister came to town; the service was then attended by those who did not wish to make the often perilous three-mile journey to Paxton. And in the years before and during the French and Indian War, frequent bloody Indian raids made that trip perilous indeed. It is said that Paxton's famous "Fighting Parson," the Reverend John Elder, carried his musket into the high pulpit when he preached; the worshippers stacked theirs at the church doors under the watchful eyes of lookouts posted to warn of the approach of Indian war parties. And it was because of these raids, which occurred while the Provincial Council sat safely in Philadelphia ignoring the pleas of Elder and others for protection, that in 1763 the "Paxton Boys" massacred the hapless—and helpless—Conestogas at Conestoga and Lancaster in retaliation. Looking back from the secure vantage point of 200 years later, it seems a brutal, senseless slaughter of innocent, harmless Indians. To men who had buried the scalped, mutilated bodies of their loved ones, it was quite a different matter.

Paxton Presbyterian Church is one of Harrisburg's historic landmarks. Here John Elder served as pastor from 1738 until his death in 1792. He is buried in the churchyard, along with Harrisburg's founder, John Harris II (who preceded him by a year), Harris' son-in-law William Maclay (Pennsylvania's first United States senator), many other notables of the city's early history, and soldiers of every war from the French and Indian War to World War II.

No brief account can do justice to "Old Paxton," mother of Presbyterianism in Harrisburg. Only a visit can do that, a visit to the marker on the site of the first church, the Archives Room and the sanctuary, the replica of the log meetinghouse in the grove above the present building, the graveyard (some call it the most historic spot in the United States), and the manse.

For a generation Paxton Church was not only the first but the only *established* place of worship in what is now Greater Harrisburg. It counted among its members most of the men whose names are associated with the city's early history. Considerably later came the first churches in the town that John Harris II commissioned William Maclay to lay out, forty-five years after John Elder's congregation erected their austere gray stone church in the wilds three miles to the east.

The distinction of being the first organized church in Harrisburg proper belongs to the present Salem United Church of Christ, at Third and Chestnut streets. In planning the town, Harris and Maclay provided a lot at this location for the erection of a church. Two years later, in March 1787, a subscription list was circulated to secure funds for that purpose. A log meetinghouse was built on a lot having a 35-foot frontage on Chestnut Street and a 39-foot depth along Cherry Alley. The church was built on the rear of the lot at South Third Street and Cherry Alley. Both Evangelical Lutheran and German Reformed worshippers had subscribed, and the two denominations united in their use of the building until 1814.

By that time the two groups had grown to such an extent that the log meetinghouse was no longer adequate. The Lutherans then purchased a lot on Fourth Street, between Chestnut and Market, and erected the Zion Lutheran Church, dedicating it on October 1, 1815. In a successor to this church, on December 4, 1839, the Whig party met in national convention and nominated William Henry Harrison for President and John Tyler for Vice President. They won with the famous "Tippecanoe and Tyler too" slogan—referring to Harrison's famous victory over the Indians. Harrison died after one month as President. (Incidentally, Harrisburg is the smallest city ever to play host to a national political convention.)

In 1816 the Lutherans sold their inter-

This old pen-and-ink drawing of a funeral procession about to enter Harrisburg's first Zion Lutheran Church dates back to the early nineteenth century.

The church was built in 1814-15 by a congregation which formerly worshipped with their German Reformed brethren in the old log church nearby. On October 21, 1838, it was destroyed by fire. Undaunted, the Lutherans built on the same site the present structure, which has been altered several times during the intervening years.

Local residents of the Catholic faith erected their first church in 1826-27, on the north side of State Street, between Second and Third. Pictured above in an early pen and ink sketch by an unknown artist, it was then under the direction of the Rev. Father Curran.

Today a magnificent cathedral, built 1904-07 occupies the same site. It is interesting to note that Harrisburg has been the seat of an area diocese since 1868.

est in the original Chestnut Street property to the German Reformed group, and on this and the adjoining lot the German Reformed Salem Church was built in 1818. Three years later the congregation voted to erect a new building; it was dedicated August 4, 1822. Later it was renamed Salem United Church of Christ. An established historic Harrisburg landmark, and now included in the National Register of Historic Places, the church rallied support to defeat plans to take over and raze it in the early 1970's as part of the modern "improvements" of downtown Harrisburg.

These were the earliest of Harrisburg's churches. As the city's population grew, with an increasing diversification of denominations, other churches were built in rapid succession to accommodate them. The construction of the Pennsylvania Canal, for which the labor force was largely Irish, increased the Catholic population in the city; St.

Presbyterians in the Harrisburg area worshipped at Paxtang until 1796, when a local congregation was formed under the leadership of Rev. Nathaniel Snowden. Before the first court house was built they held services in the loft of the old log jail. Later they moved their meetings to the first permanent court house, and in 1804 purchased a lot on South Second Street, where the church pictured above was built in 1808. Later a congregation split caused formation of the Pine Street Church. The Second Street edifice was destroyed by fire in 1858, and in 1860 the congregation moved to Market Square, where it has remained ever since.

Patrick's was erected in 1826 and dedicated in October of the following year. Located on State Street, between Second and Third, it has since been enlarged and improved.

Next, chronologically, was the Protestant Episcopal Church. Previously Episcopal worshippers had used the old log meetinghouse on Third Street and Cherry Alley. Formally organized in 1826, the congregation erected St. Stephen's on Front Street below Pine in 1827. It was long noted as having the finest bell and organ in what was then the borough of Harrisburg. The church, little changed externally, is another of the city's historic buildings.

In this sketch of early Harrisburg, it is not intended to consider more than its oldest churches and their buildings. To include details concerning later ones up to the 1860's would require in itself another book. Mention must be made, however, of some of the many. Among them is Grace Methodist Episcopal Church—now Grace United Methodist Church—on State Street between Second and Third. This church served as the meeting place of the State Assembly following the burning of the old capitol in 1897. The humorous comment was made then that this was the first time that the legislators could be gotten together in a house of worship.

Market Square Presbyterian Church and Pine Street Presbyterian Church at

Third and Pine, at their present locations after various vicissitudes including fire and relocation, are fine examples of mid-nineteenth-century church architecture. Both are offshoots of "Old Paxton."

The Baptists organized early—in 1830; even earlier—in 1827—a branch of the German Reformed Church organized into "The Church of God" under the pastorate of the Reverend John Winebrenner. Harrisburg was thus the birthplace of a new denomination, one now an established religious element in the community. For a long time worshippers of this denomination were known as "Winebrennarians," much to the stern disapproval of its founder.

A listing of all of Harrisburg's places of worship today would probably name over a hundred churches, chapels, and assemblies, evidence that the city's religious growth has kept pace with its burgeoning population and industry. If "Where there is no vision, the people perish" be true, then Harrisburg may look forward to an even richer life in the future.

Another of the city's old buildings still in existence is that at Second and South streets. Built in 1820 by a Methodist congregation, it later served a United Brethren group which only used it for a few years before turning it over to an organization that called itself "The Sons of Temperance." In the early years of this century it was purchased and used for many years by the Ohev Sholem congregation. In the 1930s it again changed hands when the congregation moved to a new temple at Front and Seneca streets. Since that time it has been utilized as a store and office building.

Enraged by the numerous attacks upon white settlers by marauding bands of Indian warriors in this area, a group of farmers residing in the Paxtang area formed a band to avenge the atrocities. Calling themselves "The Paxtonians," they were promptly nicknamed "The Paxton Boys." On December 27, 1763, ignoring the pleas of Rev. John Elder, they attacked the Lancaster County Jail, where a group of Conestoga Indians were being held in protective custody, and killed all of them, including women and children. Reproduced here is an artist's conception of the notorious event.

Perilous Times,

Chapter 4

No history of early Harrisburg would be complete without at least a brief mention of the famous Paxton Boys and their massacre of the Indians at Conestoga and Lancaster in 1763. The whole subject is controversial; there was disagreement then among some—as there is today among local historians—as to the justification for what on the face of it was a brutal slaughter.

To try to understand, one must know the circumstances that led up to it. What was life like then on the Pennsylvania frontier?

Up to the time when English and French rivalry in the New World flared into open war in 1754—that part of the Seven Years' War known as the French and Indian War—relations with the In-

the Paxton Boys, and the Revolution

dians had been comparatively peaceful at Harris Ferry on the lower Susquehanna. But during those years before 1754 the steady advance of English settlers had been driving the Indians westward toward the Ohio Valley, where the already established French began turning the dispossessed Shawnees and Delawares against their former English friends. A reign of terror began that lasted for more than forty years, ending only when Pennsylvania-born General "Mad Anthony" Wayne decisively defeated the Indians at Fallen Timbers and dictated the Treaty of Greenville (Ohio) in 1795.

During those dark years the Indian raids on the defenseless settlers at Paxtang, Derry, Donegal, and the scattered farms near Harris Ferry made life a nightmare. Almost daily some isolated cabin or tiny settlement knew the terror of murderous attack, with scalping, mutilation, and the carrying away of women and children into captivity. Repeated pleading letters from Harris, Parson Elder, and others to the Colonial Assembly at Philadelphia brought no assistance or protection. Harris himself barely escaped death as he and a party of forty men were returning from the scene of a massacre at Penn's Creek, where they had gone to bury the dead.

Forced to rely upon themselves, the settlers around Paxton formed a band of mounted rangers and elected their pastor colonel. But the farmer-rangers could not guard all points; the murderous raids continued, and the frustrated rage of the settlers mounted at each atrocity. Finally a ranger came on the scene of an attack too late to aid the slaughtered victims, but in time to track the killers to the peaceful Indian village at Conestoga. His report was all the Paxton Boys needed; it was the spark that kindled the fire. Armed and mounted, they called on their fifty-seven-year-old pastor-colonel to lead them. He protested, pointing out that the Conestogas

were few and friendly, that in an attack the rangers could not distinguish between innocent and guilty.

But there was no stopping the determined men. This quote from an old account: " 'Innocent! Can they be called innocent who foster murderers?' Mr. Elder rode up in front, and said, 'As your pastor, I command you to relinquish your design.' 'Give way then,' said one Smith, 'or your horse dies,' presenting his rifle. To save his horse, to which he was much attached, Mr. Elder drew him aside, and the Rangers were off on their fatal errand.''

So on the night of December 14, 1763, the frontier rangers of Paxton and Donegal, numbering, according to reports, from twenty to fifty, set out on their mission of vengeance. Arriving at Conestoga in the cold darkness of early dawn they swooped down on the sleeping village. Most of the men were away hunting, or trading in Lancaster; the few remaining tried to fight back, but the entire village—men, women, and children—died under the rifles, tomahawks, and knives of the attackers. The village was burned and the Paxton Boys returned to their homes.

Outraged at the slaughter, citizens and officials of Lancaster gathered in the scattered members of the tribe and gave them refuge in the stone workhouse, under guard. Learning of this, the Paxton Boys came again by night, hiding on the outskirts of Lancaster. The next day, (Sunday, December 27), they dashed into town while the town folk were at worship, forced the workhouse, and slaughtered its fourteen helpless occupants. Two of the Indians killed were recognized as members of the raiding party who had been tracked to Conestoga.

Now fully aroused and encouraged by their success, a large number of rangers from Paxton and neighboring communities marched on Philadelphia in early January, determined to wipe out the Indian population there. The alarmed Philadelphians prepared riflemen, horsemen, and even artillery to resist them. The Paxton Boys discreetly withdrew.

But they had accomplished their main purpose. A Mr. Smith, one of the rangers (perhaps the Smith who had threatened to kill Parson Elder's horse), summed it up in the account he wrote later of the Paxton Boys' exploits: "This gave quiet to the frontiers, for no murder of our defenceless inhabitants has since happened."

In spite of the indignant governor's proclamation denouncing the rangers and offering a reward for their apprehension, local public opinion was such that, although the raiders made no effort to conceal their participation, not one was ever arrested. According to Elder, himself, most of them were highly respected members of the church and community who had been goaded beyond the point of Christian forgiveness by the outrages they had suffered at the hands of savage enemies.

The French and Indian War had been over for only a few years before England, now secure in her hold on the New World, began to exploit her American colonies. "Taxation without representation," colonial trade restrictions, and an overall arrogant disregard for colonists' rights fanned flames of resentment among a people, largely English, who in this new land had developed a fiercer love of liberty than their counterparts in the British Isles.

At the first agitation for independence, John Harris was reluctant to favor it; he thought the colonies were too weak to win. But with the Declaration he made his decision. As a practical man, knowing that wars can't be fought without money, he turned over to the new Continental treasury £3,000 for certificates which he later was obliged to sell at a loss. Three of his sons served as officers in the army, and one—John

III—was reported to have died in Benedict Arnold's ill-fated attack on Quebec, December 31, 1775. Though Harris stayed at home, he was active in procuring military supplies and arranged for their transport. In fact, it appears that Harris Ferry became an important supply depot for the American army.

The men of Harris Ferry district did their share. One of the earliest companies of riflemen in the colonies was raised here and led by Captain Matthew Smith. This company formed part of the command of Daniel Morgan through the unbelievable hardships of the march to Quebec, and served during the rest of the war with that redoubtable leader. Morgan's command was a picked group: every man had to qualify as an expert marksman. Armed with Pennsylvania rifles (often erroneously called Kentucky rifles), they could literally shoot the eye out of a treed squirrel. The accuracy of Morgan's riflemen in picking off British officers helped to decide the American victory at Saratoga, which resulted in Burgoyne's surrender of his invading army.

Another company, recruited in the Harrisburg area by Captain John Murray in March 1776, saw action under Washington in the battles of Long Island, Brandywine, Trenton, White Plains, and Princeton. Many of today's Harrisburgers can find their ancestors' names on the rolls of these and other companies from this locality.

The Ferry settlement not only sent out men to war, but was also a haven of refuge for the victims of war. In 1778 it sheltered the survivors of the Wyoming Valley massacre, and on other occasions gave shelter to victims of British-led Indian attacks on the settlements to the north. All in all, though no Revolutionary War battles were fought in its vicinity, there is ample evidence that the community faithfully shared in the common cause and did its part in winning American independence.

Market day in Market Square on a sunny day in the 1870s. This scene was repeated regularly from the 1790s until 1889, when the market sheds were pulled down. The photo was taken by one of Harrisburg's early professional photographers, LeRue Lemer, 206 Market Street. Note the horse car tracks of the Harrisburg City Passenger Railway curving around the twin market houses.

Boroughood

Chapter 5

As Harrisburg's centennial year approaches, following so closely the nation's 200th anniversary, the detailing of the year-by-year growth of the community would be an impossible task and outside the scope of this book. Instead, and somewhat in almanac fashion, this chapter endeavors to provide an overview of Harrisburg, covering roughly the period from its elevation into borough status on April 13, 1791 to about 1810.

The original bounds of the borough are, of course, a matter of record, though today it would be impossible to

A controversial figure in state and national politics and the business world, General Simon Cameron left his mark on the local scene. A street and a municipal parkway are named for him.

Active in political organizing, he served—during a long life—as Adjutant-General of Pennsylvania Militia, U.S. Senator (three and a half terms), Secretary of War for a year under Pres. Lincoln, plus a stint as Ambassador to Russia.

In business his career was also varied and most successful. Early in life he was a newspaper publisher and official state printer dabbling in politics. As a result he and a brother got into the canal-building business, graduating from there to banking, railroad construction, and then to iron furnace operations.

While in Harrisburg he lived at 223 Market Street, later moving to Middletown where he died in 1889 at the ripe age of 90.

The former Cameron mansion in South Harrisburg was built by a son, James Donald, whose family later donated it and the adjoining acreage to the city for a park.

trace them exactly. The surveyor started at low water mark on the river at a *pineapple tree*, proceeded northeast to an ash tree on the west bank of Paxton Creek, followed the creek in a general way to "a white hickory on William Maclay's line" (approximately to present South Street), then went southwest "to a marked chestnut-oak" on the riverbank, and back to the starting point. Thus the borough originally was—very roughly—a long rectangle (mathematicians might suggest a

trapezoid) bounded on the west by the river.

In 1838 the borough was extended to the north along the river "to the upper line of the land of the late William Maclay."

In the early days there was a pond in the eastern section of Market Square, used for skating in the winter and as a place for frog hunting by boys in the summer. It emptied into the river at about Walnut Street. For a long time there was a densely grown swamp—called Maclay's Swamp—in the low ground between present Second and Third streets, from Pine to North Street. Another large swamp covered much of the area east and northeast of Second Street; it also was the scene of winter skating and in summer was a place for hunting frogs and snapping turtles. In those days there was nothing but forest

Samuel S. Rutherford (1803-72), a son of Thomas and Jean Rutherford, early settlers at Paxtang, was active in civic affairs of the Harrisburg area for many years. He was a farmer residing on the family estate and great-grandfather of Mrs. Henry K. Hamilton, the former Suzanne Rutherford, a resident of Paxtang.

and small natural meadows to the east beyond present Market and Fifth streets.

With the end of the Revolutionary War and with boroughhood ''just around the corner'' one may properly begin a Harrisburg almanac of the period.

FLOODS

Harrisburg has had its share of floods, more, it is believed, than have been recorded for posterity. The first recorded was in 1744, the next in 1758, followed by one in 1772. Then in 1784 occurred what became known as the Great Ice Flood, when a sudden January thaw after a bitter winter melted the deep snow in the upper river valley. The swollen river burst through the ice, sending down huge cakes. Another freezing spell stopped the flow until a March thaw sent water and enormous fragments of ice dams on a course of destruction, battering houses to fragments and carrying away the pieces.

The first court at Harris Ferry was held in a log house at the corner of Front and Washington streets. Later sessions were held in another log building at Market and Dewberry until the brick structure pictured above was erected (1792-99) on the site of the present S. S. Kresge store. It remained in use until 1860, when a larger structure replaced it. In 1948 the County Court moved again, this time to handsome headquarters at Front and Market streets.

Mary A. Rutherford, wife of Samuel S. Rutherford, who shared her husband's interest in the affairs of the community in which she lived over a long period of years.

Children of early settlers in Harrisburg were tutored mainly by private teachers until the erection of a log school at Third and Walnut streets shortly after the town was laid out. In 1828 the commissioners of Dauphin County authorized the construction of a large brick building on Walnut Street at Aberdeen Street, the site of City Hall as of 1976. In 1848 it was purchased by the North Ward School Board. First named the Lancasterian School, its name later was changed to the Dewitt Building. It remained in use until 1910, when it was torn down to make way for Harrisburg Technical High School. During the Civil War it was pressed into use as a temporary army hospital, and afterwards became the city's first high school.

Two years later, in September 1786, came the Great Pumpkin Flood, when thousands of pumpkins washed out of the farmers' fields in the upper Susquehanna and literally covered the ground at Harris Ferry when the waters receded. A sixth flood battered the community in the spring of 1800, another in August, 1814, and an eighth in the same month in 1817. After a respite of almost a generation, the Susquehanna sent down a tremendous flood in the spring of 1846 which carried away the eastern end of Camelback Bridge and part of the Cumberland Valley Railroad bridge.

WILD ANIMALS

In the 1780's it was not unusual for bears, wolves, wild turkeys, and deer to appear on the outskirts of the town, or even invade the settlement. On one occasion in 1792, a buffalo joined a herd of cows pastured in Maclay's Swamp and stampeded them into the town before it was finally killed in Harris' stable in River Alley. That buffalo may have been one of the last of the eastern woods buffaloes. And for years the river islands were nesting places for numbers of bald eagles which fed in the spring on the shad ascending the river to spawn.

HARRISBURG: CAPITAL OF THE UNITED STATES?

It may come as a surprise to the reader to learn that the community was once seriously considered as the site for the national government. Following the close of the Revolutionary War, the question of a permanent seat of government was debated in Congress. Finally, in 1789, the Congress then in session in New York began an earnest consideration of the question. Naturally each section wished for the honor, but a com-

promise agreement was reached providing that the permanent national capital should "be fixed as near the centre of wealth, population and extent of territory" as would be practicable. That pointed to Pennsylvania, the "Keystone State," and a further narrowing down fixed the location "on the east bank of the Susquehanna river."

A Pennsylvania representative offered an amendment adding "between Harrisburg and Middletown, inclusive" after the word "river." On a vote the southern states defeated the amendment, but Pennsylvania was still in the running. In its 1790 session Congress again considered the problem. Sectional feeling was now so strong that an unsuccessful effort was made to compromise, but finally a few northern votes were changed and the bill of the previous session was passed, with the substitution of Potomac for Susquehanna. Possibly few Harrisburgers now grieve at this loss.

THE FIRST COURT

The first court in Dauphin County was held at Harris Ferry on the third Tuesday in May, 1785, in a log house at the corner of Front and Washington streets. Later courts occupied the log jail on Strawberry Alley, and a log house on Market Street near Dewberry Alley. After several other moves the courts finally acquired a permanent home when the Dauphin County Court House was built on the north side of Market Street at Court Street, between Second and Third. There it remained until recent years, when the erection of the splendid building at Front and Market streets gave the county courts their present home. Two pillars from the colonnade of the old Market Street Court House now stand at the Eighteenth Street entrance to Reservoir Park.

Said to be the oldest house still standing within the city limits is that built by the Rev. John Elder, early pastor of Paxton Presbyterian Church. The handsome stone residence, now located at 2426 Ellerslie Street, has undergone a number of renovations over the years. Date stones embedded in the walls record the construction date (1740) and that of the first alteration (1829). The photograph was taken in 1960.

An 1880 photo of the western section of Theodore Burr's famous Camelback Bridge. It was completed in 1817 and survived storms and floods until 1902. The almost dry river bed indicates low water conditions prevailing opposite the city before the Dock Street dam was built.

THE FIRST DAUPHIN COUNTY COMMISSIONERS

These first commissioners all bore names associated with the early development of Harrisburg. Again and again in the records of those times appear the names of Jacob Awl, William Brown, James Cowden, Joshua Elder, and Andrew Stewart. Descendants of some still figure in the life of Harrisburg today.

MARKET SQUARE AND MARKET STREET

These were appropriately named. As early as 1807 small market houses were erected in the Square; there townspeople could buy meat and vegetables brought in by farmers from the surrounding area. These market houses later were made larger, and on market days the Square presented a busy sight with its throngs of shoppers and crowded ranks of farm wagons. When progress dictated the removal of the market in 1889, Harrisburg did not have to give up its "going to the market" habit. Neighborhood markets had already been established: West Harrisburg Market House "uptown" at Broad and Third (1860), East Harrisburg Farmers' Market in the Allison Hill section at Market Street and Fourteenth (1873), and the State Street Market at Fourth and State (1872). Two new markets also appeared in the same year that the market on the Square was removed: Chestnut Street Market at Chestnut and Court streets, and the Kelker Street Market at Kelker and Fourth.

The first of these five, officially named the Verbeke Street Market but universally called Broad Street Market, is one of Harrisburg's four entries in the National Register of Historic Places. The other three are the John Harris Mansion, the Walnut Street bridge, and Salem Church.

THE GREAT SICKNESS

In 1793, the year of the yellow fever epidemic in Philadelphia, a virulent fever of a similar nature attacked Harrisburg. Fearful that infected people from Philadelphia might intensify the epidemic, the town authorities posted patrols at the southern end of town to halt travelers. In casting about for the cause of the sickness, citizens seized upon the idea that the "miasma" from a mill dam on Paxton Creek was carrying the fever. Money was raised by subscription, the dam and mill were purchased from the Landis brothers, and a committee broke open the dam, draining

The Harrisburg National Bank was organized in 1814–just thirteen years after the borough of Harrisburg was created by an act of the Legislature. It opened for business at 9 A.M., July 6, 1814, in the parlor of its cashier, Mr. John Downey, who resided on South Second Street, directly opposite the then new Presbyterian church. Three years later it moved into a building on Market Square which was replaced in 1854 by the one pictured here. This, in turn, was razed in 1974 to make way for the large multipurpose building now occupying almost half a city block.

a pond of eight to ten acres. Three of the five county commissioners' names appeared on the subscription list: Jacob Awl, Joshua Elder, and Andrew Stewart.

FIRST NEWSPAPER

First newspaper in Harrisburg was *The Harrisburg Journal and Weekly Advertiser*. It made its appearance in 1789 under the editorship of T. Roberts. It was, as its name stated, a weekly; it was printed in single folio. In 1792 John Wyeth took over the paper and renamed it *The Oracle of Dauphin and Harrisburg Advertiser*. It flourished under Wyeth family management until 1840 as a powerful influence in the community. The Wyeths also did some book and pamphlet publishing. Historians of early Harrisburg owe much to *The Oracle* in their reconstruction of the town's first fifty years.

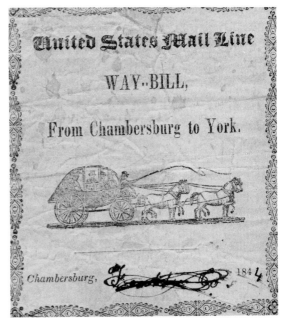

Typical of the waybills issued for the transportation of mail and parcels by Harrisburg's stage line operator William Calder is this reproduction of an old copy (1844) now preserved in the State Archives.

Harrisburg was an important stop for overland travel long before the advent of canal and railroad. Stagecoaches and Conestoga wagons as shown in this painting by John W. Storm, displayed in the Pennsylvania Department of Internal Affairs, were a common sight in Harris Ferry town before it became a city.

Following an epidemic of typhoid fever in the late 1790s, Harrisburg got its first water supply system. A reservoir was built on the elevation north of the site of the first Capitol bordering North Street. It had a capacity of 1,532,195 gallons pumped up from the river with the aid of a primitive steam-driven pump. This engraving shows how the city's Mt. Airy Water Works looked in 1840.

John Harris stored military supplies at his trading post, and from that time on Harrisburg has served as a storage and distribution center for the nation's armed forces. Above is an old woodcut depicting the first United States Arsenal here, located just east of the first Capitol, as it looked in 1857.

John Wyeth, Harrisburg's third postmaster, was also active in other fields of endeavor. He was publisher of The Oracle of Dauphin *and* The Harrisburg Advertiser *newspapers, gave the town its first theater, and was prominent in local government and civic affairs for many years.*

His first mail carrier, Benjamin A. Taylor, rode a mail delivery route on horseback as far as Alexandria in Huntingdon County. This made a round trip of 216 miles every week. Local people called at *The Oracle* for their mail; it was a favorite place for exchange of news in those leisurely days, and Postmaster Wyeth was thus enabled to garner many local items for Editor Wyeth.

HARRIS FAMILY

On March 23, 1795, four years after the death of John Harris II and his burial in Paxton Churchyard, *The Oracle* carried an advertisement offering the ferry operation "to be let, for the term of one year."

Just a month earlier, Harris' son, David, had offered his family home for rent. The description of the property as it was then is of interest: "large lot and stone house, built of the best materials, containing four spacious rooms on the first story, with fire-places in each, and six rooms on the second, with a large stone kitchen, and a stable which will contain thirty or forty horses . . . an excellent cellar under the whole house, divided into three apartments, with vaults . . . ."

The Harris Mansion was built in 1766. (Parson John Elder's home, built in 1740, is the present city's oldest.) After the death of the second John Harris it was rented until 1863, when it was purchased by Simon Cameron, Pennsylvania's political boss and Lincoln's first secretary of war. Cameron made some changes, among them lowering the first floor three feet, and relandscaping the grounds. The latest owner is the Dauphin County Historical Society, in-

THE WHISKEY REBELLION

Harrisburg had its share of excitement in this early testing of the authority of the national government. The Second Pennsylvania Regiment, mostly Harrisburgers, was mustered for service but appears not to have been used. One company of volunteers, however, did march as far as Carlisle before the Rebellion ended. For Harrisburg the memorable event of the Rebellion occurred on October 4, 1794 with the arrival of President and Commander in Chief George Washington, on his way west. He was greeted with an address by the burgesses and responded graciously. He lodged overnight at a tavern on the east corner of the Square and Market Street, where the historic Jones House later stood.

FIRST POSTMASTER

This was John Wyeth, editor of *The Oracle*. His bookstore on Second Street near Mulberry served as the post office.

One of the city's early places of learning was the Harrisburg Academy, incorporated in April of 1809. About 1816 the students and faculty moved into and occupied a section of the historic William Maclay Mansion, Front and South Streets. By the year 1847 the Academy had outgrown its quarters and the building pictured here next door to the Maclay house was erected. Many years later the school was moved to a beautiful campus north of Harrisburg in the community of Riverside. Today the Harrisburg Academy continues its role as an educational institution of the West Shore, between Wormleysburg and Camp Hill.

corporated in 1869. In the Society's rooms in the old mansion are preserved many fascinating memorabilia of Harrisburg's and Dauphin County's early history.

RIVER IMPROVEMENT

With Harrisburg a rapidly growing town in 1795, the river was considered one of the main means of transport to and from the community. In August of that year measures were undertaken to finance the removal of rocks and other obstructions in the river between the mouths of Swatara Creek and the Juniata, and between Wright's Ferry (Wrightsville) and the Maryland line.

LIBRARY

"The Mechanical Society of Harrisburg" originated in 1794; the following year the "Harrisburg Library Company" was organized from this society. The Library Company functioned until 1813, then disposed of its books by lot-tery. In 1830 the Harrisburg Library Association was formed; it was replaced in 1889 by the Harrisburg Public Library Association now housed—thanks to the Haldeman-Haly Foundation—in the beautiful stone building on the corner of Front and Walnut streets. This library and the magnificent State Library provide Harrisburg with an unsurpassed wealth of reading material for entertainment, instruction, and research.

THEATER

In Harrisburg theater began early. On September 12, 1796, *The Oracle* announced a performance by The Harrisburg Company of Comedians. They were amateurs—"a number of young gentlemen of this town." Now theater in Harrisburg has come full circle; after nearly a century and a half of professional drama by touring and stock companies, the city's theaters are gone and playgoers must turn to an excellent Community Theater and its talented amateurs.

The first permanent theater in the borough of Harrisburg was built by John Wyeth at the corner of Locust and Court streets in 1841. It was originally named Shakespeare Hall and served the community for many years in various capacities before being razed in 1910 to make way for the present Telegraph Building.

The Harrisburg, Portsmouth, Mt. Joy & Lancaster Railroad provided shelter for its passengers and even refreshments from a pie stand in the city's first railroad station, constructed in 1837. The drawing shows the station after it was leased by the infant Pennsylvania Railroad in 1847. It was replaced by a much larger structure in 1857. Thirty years later the present building, scheduled for renovation as part of the Harristown plan, was erected, and this too has seen many changes during the intervening years. All three stations occupied virtually the same location. The station built in 1887 has been designated a National Historic Landmark. The building will remain in use as a transportation center.

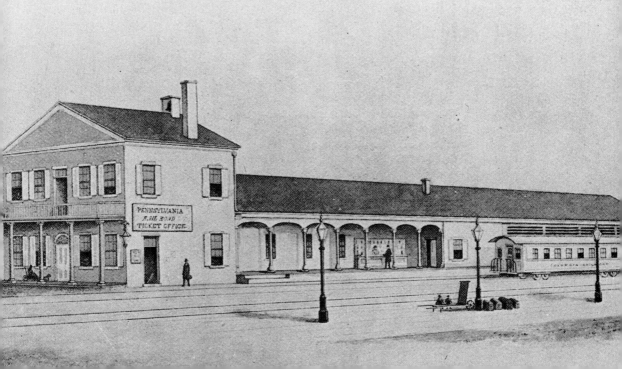

WEATHER

On September 26, 1796 *The Oracle* forecast a hard winter, basing its prediction on the huge number of squirrels crossing the river ice from Cumberland County to Harrisburg. Some citizens killed and salted *"barrels* of them for their winter's use."

It is often argued that contemporary winters are not as long, cold, and snowy as they were in "the good old days." One of the authors can supply a bit of ammunition for that argument. His wife's father, John Geiger Ingram, born in 1870 at 113 Market Street, often told his daughter that as a small boy he saw buggies and light farm carts crossing the river on the ice at Thanksgiving time.

DEATH OF GEORGE WASHINGTON

The Oracle appeared with black mourning borders on December 30, 1799, to announce the death of the nation's first President. Prominent citizens met to pass resolutions of regret at his passing, and most Harrisburgers wore mourning bands during the following month.

EARTHQUAKE

Not to be outdone by California, Alaska, and the Carolinas, Harrisburg experienced two earthquake shocks on November 20, 1800. The first brought people from their beds at 4:45 in the morning and lasted about forty seconds, rattling doors and breaking chinaware. The second came twenty minutes later, continuing for half a minute. A distinct rumbling noise was heard during both tremors. This was on a Thursday; there is no record of whether church attendance was greater on the following Sunday!

STAGE LINES

In October of 1808 advertisements began to appear in *The Oracle* for a once-a-week Harrisburg and Philadelphia stage line, and a mail stage which ran weekly to Alexandria, Huntingdon County, for a $6 fare. This apparently eliminated the mail rider's job mentioned earlier. The instituting of stage lines was a sure indication of the growing importance of Harrisburg.

Imposing was the main entrance to the Commonwealth's first permanent seat of government. This is how it looked in 1890. Later, prior to its destruction by fire, the walkway leading to the portico was widened and the unsightly pole with its strange-looking electric arc light removed.

The Harrisburg Nail Works (located across the river in West Fairview) was built about 1833 by Gabriel Hiester, a brother of Gov. Joseph Hiester, who is said to have built a home on Front Street, West Fairview, in 1823. The industry assisted the economy of the area for many years, being abandoned in the early 1900s and torn down about 1911.

Another of the city's collection of old residences still standing is the Maclay Mansion at Front and South streets. It was built in 1790 by William Maclay, son-in-law of the city's founder. Maclay laid out the town in 1785 and became one of its prominent citizens. Much altered in appearance, the sturdy stone building is presently owned by the Pennsylvania Bar Association. The other building in the photograph, taken many years ago, was the first home of the Harrisburg Academy, erected in 1847.

Second president of Harrisburg's Dauphin Deposit Trust Co. was James McCormick, who held that office for thirty years prior to his death in 1870. He was succeeded in turn by two sons, Henry (1870-74) and James (1874-1908). A grandson of the first president, Donald McCormick took charge in 1912 and continued until 1945.

The first James McCormick was born in Cumberland County in 1801, and in 1825 was admitted to the bar after studying law at Princeton. Later he served as a member of Harrisburg Borough Council and was elected head of the bank in 1840. For many years he was associated with the Harrisburg Bridge Company, the Harrisburg Cemetery, and was an active member of the Pine Street Presbyterian Church. Upon retirement he took over the management of his large family estate, consisting of iron furnaces, rolling mills, grist mills and farms.

SCHOOLS

Advertisements in October and November, 1808, by individuals seeking to open private schools indicated a movement away from the church-conducted schools that were characteristic of earliest Harrisburg. The next step would be the beginning of a public school system.

In February 1809 the public was invited to the opening "of the new Presbyterian Church, in Second Street" (forerunner of the present Market Square Church). In the same month a German-language newspaper, *the Volksfreund*, was proposed by Messrs. Albright, Ehrenfried, and Hamilton.

In late February and early March 1809 the legislature took the first steps toward establishing Harrisburg as the permanent capital of Pennsylvania.

April 1809 saw the incorporation of the company that was to employ Theodore Burr to design and construct the city's famous Camelback Bridge in 1811.

The first bank in the borough was a branch of the Philadelphia Bank. Beginning operations in May, 1809, it was located on the southwest corner of the Square, where the later Harrisburg Bank stood. In October the borough employed the bank's watchman as a night patrolman at an additional salary.

In December of that year the Harris ferry operation was again advertised for rent.

February 1810 became the month in which Harrisburg was officially named capital of the state.

About this time (1810 or 1811) Harrisburg received its first shipment of anthracite coal. It came from Wilkes-Barre in a river "ark." The entire cargo was sold to merchant Jacob Boas. The size of the town at that time may be deduced from the assertion then that the coal was more than enough to supply the needs of Harrisburg for one year. Obviously, it wasn't intended solely for heating!

Although these "almanac notes" of Harrisburg events progress only to 1810, there remain two other items curiously indicative of the period.

April 20, 1811. *Oracle* publisher John Wyeth advertised "a Circulating Library, charging . . . six cents per volume for perusing duodecimos and ten cents for octavos."

June 2, 1811, *The Oracle* quoted the following: "*Riflemen Attention!* A man to be shot for the benefit of his wife and children—$1 a shot, one hundred yards distance, with rifles—on Wednesday, the 13th inst., at Govanstown, at 3 p.m.

The above mentioned man is in a very low state of health, and wishes to leave his family snug.''

William Calder's livery stable office was located at 16-18 North Market Square before Harrisburg gained the status of a city. Calder, who at one time operated extensive stagecoach routes out of Harrisburg, maintained his equipment and horses at the rear of the property shown here. The photo was taken in 1869; the gentleman leaning on the hitching post is City Controller Larue Metzgar.

The Senate Chamber of Pennsylvania's first Capitol as it appeared in the 1850s is illustrated above in a reproduction of a well-executed steel engraving. According to partial information accompanying it, the Speaker of the Senate at that time was W. M. Hiester, representing Berks County. Seated at the extreme right in front of a window was J. G. Shuman, of Lancaster County, and the senator on the extreme left was William Piatt, Wyoming County.

The arrow at the bottom of this old picture points to the site of the first post office to be established in Harrisburg. The location: 202 South Second Street, in the building later occupied by D. F. Jauss, dealer in stoves and tinware. This picture was taken in the 1890s.

Many old homes in the city survived a long time in altered form. Such was 113 Market Street, built 1814-15 by John Fager and purchased from him by George Geiger.

Mr. Geiger's sister, Malvina, operated a store in the front room of their home and married Samuel Ingram, a teacher in the city schools, who later became county superintendent of schools.

The Ingrams were the grandparents of Mrs. Robert Hoffsommer, 728 North Twenty-eighth Street, who provided the 1870 photograph.

State officials early recognized the need for an institution to care for mentally ill citizens. Consequently the Legislature authorized the establishment of a State Hospital for the Insane, only they called it a "lunatic asylum" in those days. The first unit of the present hospital, pictured here, was opened in 1851, nine years before Harrisburg became a city.

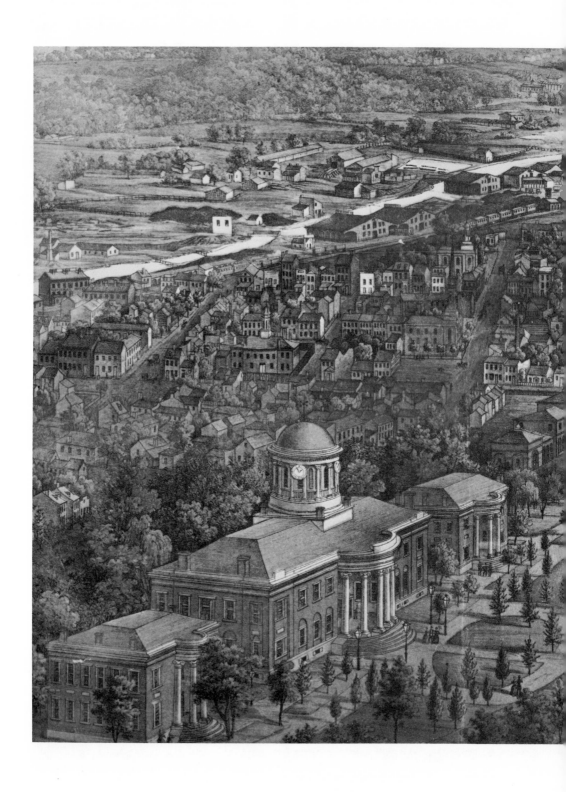

Chapter 6

From Borough to City

It is easy—too easy, in fact—for a town's annalist to concentrate on the life of his community as a detached microcosm. It *is* a little world in itself, but it is also more than that. To broadly paraphrase John Donne's famous line: No city is an island, complete in itself. It touches and influences the world about it and is in turn touched and affected by the world, in greater or lesser degree. This chapter will try to record both aspects of Harrisburg's life: the growth and changes in the city itself (some of which we have already touched upon), and the agencies by which it has been related to the world outside. These will be the river with its lumber rafting traffic, the Pennsylvania Canal, the railroads and later highways that made Harrisburg a hub of commerce, its share in the nation's wars, and its industries,

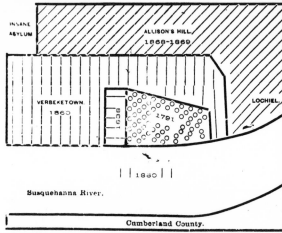

some of them short-lived but all contributing to make the Harrisburg of today.

The topography of Harrisburg had much to do with its early history and in some respects still does, especially in the matter of the floods which have plagued the community up to the present day. The growth of the town has had the effect of obliterating many minor geographical features; it should be interesting to picture the land as it appeared to Harrisburgers during the years before the borough became a city in 1860.

It was a wetter town then than it is now. A slight, gradually descending ridge constituted the riverbank to below the Harris home. There, in present South Harrisburg, the land became so low that any real rise in the river posed a flood threat. North of this, the ground dipped slightly from present Front Street to Second Street and Market Square. Before sewers were laid there, any heavy rain made a sizable pond in the Square, a circumstance that prompted a Lancaster newspaper to suggest jocularly, under the heading "Inland Navigation," that Harrisburg was planning "to adopt the Venetian style of visiting in gondolas." Drainage of water above the pond level was by a small ditch or "gut" down Walnut Street to the river.

East beyond Second Street the land sloped gradually to a swampy area bordering Paxton Creek, which roughly paralleled the river and to the present time helps to augment flood conditions when the river rises. North of Market Street the ground rose to the present Capitol Hill and continued north on present Sixth Street as a ridge. Another hill north of the Capitol gave sufficient elevation for the city's first reservoir. (To fill the reservoir the first "water works" was built in 1841 along the river at North Street.) Already mentioned was Maclay's Swamp, in the area be-

This diagram indicates the growth of the settlement at Harris Ferry between the years 1791 and 1870. A line surrounding the date 1791 represents the original borough limits. By an act of April 16, 1838, "Maclaysburg" was taken in. On March 19, 1860 Hargest Island (now City Island) and "Verbecktown" again increased the size of the community, and by the acts of April 22, 1868 and April 9, 1869, the "Allison's Hill" section was added.

tween the lower ground of Second and Third streets and the Sixth Street ridge.

East out Market Street and beyond Paxton Creek rose Allison's Hill, named for the original farmer-owner. Patches of forest and cultivated fields covered the hill; a small stream ran down a gully or ravine (later to be the extension of Market Street) and fed into a pond at present Thirteenth and Fourteenth streets.

The hills and ridges have not changed, except for minor surface leveling, but most of the water is gone, thanks to nature's lowering of the water table and man's installation of drainage systems.

Already noted was the creation of Harrisburg as a borough by an act of the Pennsylvania Assembly on April 13, 1791, and its incorporation as a city on March 19, 1860. Those sixty-nine years were years of growth and preparation for "The City Beautiful" that Harrisburg was to become in the present century. The events and achievements of those years are worth considering.

At this point, since "firsts" are always interesting, it should be mentioned that the first permanent house built in the new borough was John Hamilton's brick home on the corner of Front Street and Blackberry Alley. His place of business was on the Square at Market Street. It later became the Washington House, and then the historic Jones House where Abraham Lincoln stopped during his journey to Washington for his inauguration in 1861.

The borough limits at the very beginning of this period, as laid out by Harris' son-in-law, William Maclay, have already been mentioned. The boundaries five years later, on the lines of modern Harrisburg, were: north on Front Street from Mulberry to South Street, easterly approximately to Sixth and Walnut, south to Mulberry between Third and Fourth, and thence back to the starting point. By this time, as observed by French visitor Theophile Cazenove, the town had grown from the one house (Harris') to a respectable 300 dwellings. In addition it boasted from twenty-five

to thirty shops—general stores and places of business—and approximately thirty-eight inns and taverns. These last indicate not simply the obvious fact that Harrisburgers drank something besides water, but that the town was already a stopping place for more than the usual number of travelers.

In the last ten years of the eighteenth century and the first decade of the nineteenth, Harrisburg, though a growing community, was largely a self-contained one, concerned with its own development. Then in 1810 the State Legislature enacted a bill providing that by October, 1812, the capital of Pennsylvania was to be moved permanently from Lancaster to Harrisburg. The founder's dream was to be realized and his four acres of "Public Ground" were eventually to become the site of the Capitol and the office buildings of the Commonwealth.

So the Legislature came to Harris-

The second Dauphin County Prison, erected at the rear of the County Court House and facing Walnut Street, replaced a log structure of 1792 vintage in the year 1855. The grim-looking bastille, as it first appeared to Harrisburgers, is shown here in a reproduction of an old sketch.

Harrisburg's first Masonic Hall, pictured here, was erected by Perseverance Lodge, No. 21, F&AM, on the north side of Walnut Street, facing the county jail in 1827. It was also known as the Exchange Building, and was erected by architect-builder Samuel Holman. The first mayor's office was in this building, which was torn down in 1882 to make way for the city's first Federal Building. Of interest is the fact that Perseverance Lodge was chartered by the Grand Lodge on March 15, 1787, and instituted by George Washington.

burg. For ten years it met in the Dauphin County Court House at Market and Court streets. This was not the court house Harrisburg's old-timers remember, but the earlier building on the same site. An act providing for the erection of a State Capitol was passed March 18, 1816, the cost to be—in those happy, uninflated years—$135,000. Later acts providing for executive offices, arsenal, and "embellishment" of the public grounds raised the total to $275,000.

The arsenal was erected on the Capitol grounds, but it was torn down in the early 1870's; a new arsenal was built at Eighteenth and Herr Streets in 1874 and the grounds were enclosed by the iron fence which had originally surrounded the Capitol. The arsenal underwent some rebuilding in 1914-1915.

The cornerstone for the Capitol was laid on May 31, 1819, by Governor Findlay and architect and contractor Stephen Hills with appropriate ceremonies. (Unfortunately no distinguishing mark was put on the stone; when fire destroyed the Capitol in 1897 it was located only after a long search, under the ruins at the southeast corner of the building.)

The Legislature held its last session in the Court House in December 1821. On January 2, 1822, the lawmakers assembled there for the last time and marched in procession "two and two" to the new building, which was then dedicated with a prayer by the Reverend Doctor Lochman and an address by the Reverend D. Mason, principal of Dickinson College.

The building was two and a half stories high, of brick, with a curved colonnade at the main entrance, the whole surmounted by a modest dome. It was a far cry from the state's present magnificent Capitol, but during its seventy-five years it served its purpose adequately; through its portals passed men—such as Simon Cameron, Thaddeus Stevens, and Civil War Governor Andrew Curtin—whose names are famous in national as well as Pennsylvania history. Lafayette was an honored visitor in January 1825; the Legislature entertained Charles Dickens there during his American tour (he made a rather acid comment on the legislators' uncouthness and tobacco-chewing propensities); and Abraham Lincoln's body lay there for a day during the long journey to its final resting place in Springfield, Illinois.

The Legislature had been in its new home for only three years when in 1825 it attempted to expand the Capitol grounds to the west between North and South streets, from Third Street to Sweet Briar Alley in what was then known locally as the village of Maclaysburg. The project was abandoned when high prices and the unwillingness of some lot owners to sell bogged down negotiations. So the Capitol ground remained bounded on the west by Third Street.

The War of 1812 was America's second war for independence. Britain's interference with commerce at sea and her impressment of American sailors into British naval service during the early 1800s finally goaded Congress into a declaration of war on June 18, 1812. Though some parts of the country opposed the war, Harrisburg responded to Governor Snyder's call to arms. The town contributed generously in money and men. Several companies of volunteers were recruited here and from the surrounding district; they rendezvoused for formal enlistment at York, and marched from there to Baltimore when the British threatened that city. In 1813 Harrisburg celebrated with fireworks Perry's victory on Lake Erie and Harrison's defeat of the British and their Indian allies in the Battle of the Thames.

From the rosters of those volunteer companies can be compiled a list of men whose family names have been interwoven with Harrisburg's history, some even to the present day. Here is a partial enumeration: William Allison; Jacob M. Awl; Joel Bailey; James R. Boyd; C., William M., and John Carson; James and Matthew B. Cowden; Joshua, Jacob, and John Elder; John M. Forster; William Hamilton; David and Samuel Harris; Joseph and Frederick H. Hummel; John and Jacob Kunkel; Thomas McIlhenny; Luther and William Reily; and Peter, John, and Godfrey Snyder.

Up to the time of the war, traffic between Harrisburg and the west shore of the river had moved on boats and fer-

Gates were a part of the old Camelback Bridge, not to keep pedestrians and vehicles from crossing, but to halt herds of cattle being driven to market. It was part of the toll collector's job to count heads and collect the right amount of revenue from the herdsmen. A sign tacked to a center post advertises Rumford Baking Powder.

ries. Even with the war in progress plans were made to eliminate or at least ease that traffic bottleneck. The Legislature had authorized erection of a bridge as early as April, 1809; a bridge company was chartered in July, 1812, and construction of the city's famous camelback covered bridge began in earnest in 1813.

Theodore Burr, one of the great names in bridge construction, was both architect and builder. His bridge, when finally completed in 1817, was about two-thirds of a mile long and forty feet wide. Called a camelback because of its humped appearance between piers, it was completely enclosed and lighted only by narrow slits along its length. When Charles Dickens crossed the bridge to visit Harrisburg during his American tour in 1842, he recorded in his *American Notes* that "it was profoundly dark." (Incidentally, he lodged at the old Eagle Hotel, later the Bolton House, on the Square.)

There was a toll house at the Market Street end of the bridge where fixed rates for pedestrian and horse-drawn traffic were collected. Even when Confederates threatened to capture Harrisburg in Lee's invasion in 1863, the bridge authorities insisted on "business as usual," charging toll for the passage of New York State Militia sent to protect the town! The bridge was for nearly a century a Harrisburg landmark. It was repeatedly damaged by recurrent floods, but was repaired and kept in service until the predecessor of the present concrete and iron bridge replaced it in 1904. This was later widened and tolls were collected at houses on Forster's Island until May 15, 1957, when the state took over the bridge and the little books of toll tickets became collectors' items.

Harrisburg almost had a canal of its very own. In the Assembly session of 1822-1823 an act was passed "to enable the Governor to incorporate a company for making a canal and lock navigation on the waters of the Susquehanna, near the borough of Harrisburg, with power to the said company to supply the said borough with water and to insure against fire." Water for the canal was to come from the river near Stony Creek, about eight miles upriver, and be returned to the river "at the mouth of Paxton Creek."

The company organized in late 1825 with John Forster as president and Valentine Hummel as a member. A surveyor located the route of the canal, but when the Legislature a year later passed the act providing for the construction of the Pennsylvania Canal, the Harrisburg Canal plan was absorbed into the greater project. More will be said about this tremendous undertaking in chapter 7.

Water in all its uses—drinking, swimming, washing, fire fighting, power, icemaking, and transportation—has always been a major concern

Toll rates on local bridges in the area remained static for many years, as witness below. Automobiles were on the roads when the addition was made to the rates posted on Clarks Ferry Bridge. Rates were comparable with those on the Camelback span before the construction of the Walnut Street Bridge and its attendant competition.

CLARKS FERRY BRIDGE,
APRIL 1ST 1886,
RATES OF TOLL.

AUTOMOBILES		25¢
For a Carriage 4 Horses,	-	75¢
" " 2 "	-	40¢
" " 1 Horse,	-	25¢
" Each additional "	-	10¢
" Horse Rider,	-	15¢
" Passengers on Foot,	-	5¢
" Man Wheelbarrow,	-	10¢
" a Freight Wagon 4 Horses,	-	80¢
" " " 3 "	-	65¢
" " " 2 "	-	60¢
" " " 1 Horse,	-	25¢
" Cart 1 Horse,	-	20¢
" Lead Horse,	-	10¢
" Horned Cattle each,	-	5¢
" Sheep Hogs, "	-	1½¢

Time was when most water for personal use came from wells, and in the early days Harrisburg had its share, some public, some private. Methods for drawing water varied. Some wells sported pumps of many varieties. Others, like the one depicted here, were "dip" wells. A bucket attached to a rope, or chain, was lowered to the water level, where it was filled before being pulled back to the surface. The photo was taken about eighty years ago at a home along the "State Road" north of the city limits. The sun-bonneted woman and the lad with his pet dog remain unidentified.

Harrisburg was still a borough when the Cumberland Valley Railroad put up this unpretentious frame passenger station at the intersection of Fourth and Chestnut streets. Later an attractive brick station, which was gutted by fire in 1974 and razed, replaced it. The accompanying photo was taken in the early 1890s and shows the entrance to the city's first Mulberry Street Bridge.

of Harrisburg, not to mention its almost annual danger as flood. In those early days of careless sanitation and happy ignorance of germs, before the first reservoir Harrisburg got its household water from wells, springs, and streams—even the river. Fires were fought by bucket brigades and pump-and-hose carts pulled by volunteer householders who made up in enthusiastic earnestness what they lacked in professional skill. Most fires totally consumed the buildings where they started; if the amateur firemen could save the adjacent structures, they felt that their mission was successful. They had plenty of practice; most homes and shops were of wood, and stoves and fireplaces would scarcely have passed modern safety requirements.

As mentioned earlier, it was not until 1841 that Harrisburg had a municipal water system. On September 18 the borough's chief engineer, T. Erdman, proudly announced completion of the Harrisburg Water Works, with its pump

house on the riverbank at North and Front streets, and its reservoir with a 1.5 million-gallon capacity on a hill near the Capitol. About eight miles of pipe supplied the borough; for fire fighting there were in the neighborhood of 100 fire plugs.

The water of the river, with its potential for transportation, occupied Harrisburg's attention as early as 1795, when proposals were made to clear obstructions between Columbia and Northumberland. In 1823 the project was begun and the river was "improved" from the latter town down to tidewater. Three shallow-draft steamboats of the Baltimore Steamboat Company—the *Codorus,* the *Pioneer,* and the *Susquehanna*—came up the river to Harrisburg in the fall of 1825. They made several trips during the ensuing year until the explosion of the *Susquehanna*'s boiler, destroying the boat and killing two passengers, caused the company to discontinue its operations in 1826. That was the last of steamboats on the Susquehanna until 1857, when some local citizens brought a small side-wheel steamboat to Harrisburg to use for excursions. The venture was unsuccessful; at the end of the summer the boat was sold back to its original owners.

To keep pace with the borough's growth, the Harrisburg Gas Company was incorporated and began operations in 1850. The plant then was located east of the lines of the Pennsylvania Railroad, near the foot of Mulberry Street. Some six and a half miles of pipe carried gas to homes and factories, and even to the newly constructed lunatic asylum, known now as the State Hospital. Householders had to be cautioned not to blow out lights as they had been accustomed to do in extinguishing oil lamps.

Schooling began with the first churches. Scotch-Irish and Germans alike felt that secular education should go hand-in-hand with religious instruction. As soon as a church was organized and a building erected. the minister or

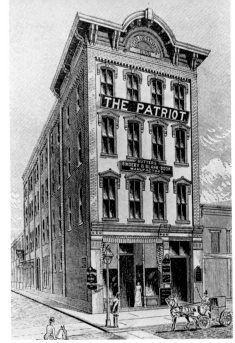

Harrisburg's morning newspaper was born in 1843 as The Democratic Union. *It later changed hands and became* The Patriot, *which was first published in a building on the southwest corner of Third and Walnut streets. In 1877 the offices and printing plant were moved into the building here depicted. Later, dictated by growth of the city and its circulation, a move was made to another building on Market Square and finally to the present quarters at 812 Market Street.*

The Pennsylvania Canal brought industrial growth to the city prior to the building of the railroads. One of the industries destined to aid the local economy for years was the big cotton mill on North Street, between Second and Front. Established in 1852, it later produced silk goods and during the Civil War doubled as an army hospital. It was torn down in the early 1930s to make way for the present YMCA and an automotive center.

some member of the congregation undertook "to teach the young idea how to shoot." Hornbooks, slates, and teaching by rote took the place of textbooks for the children. Later, as the town grew, private individuals started schools in their own homes; early issues of *The Oracle* contained numerous advertisements of such offers.

Samuel D. Ingram was a prominent educator in the young town. Coming to Harrisburg from Sunbury in 1836, he was elected in the following year to teach the Boys' Grammar School, at that time the equivalent of present-day high school. In 1844 he took over the Girls' Grammar School, teaching there for thirteen years. He was then elected first Dauphin County school superintendent and served in that capacity for fifteen years, from 1857 to 1872. Harrisburg had been divided into a North and a South Ward in 1822, and Ingram's annual report for 1858 gives some interesting statistics.

The school year then was ten months. The North Ward had fourteen schools with a teaching staff of seven men and seven women; the South Ward's ten schools were staffed by three men and seven women. In those benighted days before Women's Lib the North Ward males' monthly salaries averaged $40; the females' $27.33. Oddly, salaries averaged lower in the South Ward: $38.88 for men and $23.93 for women. North Ward schools had an enrollment of 983 scholars against 905 in the South Ward, but average attendance showed a greater disparity: 771 for the North against 610 for the South. Ingram's report shows that it cost $.49 a month then to educate one of the younger generation—something to cause

Harrisburg at one time had farms surrounding it rather than the suburbia of today. Typical of the agricultural aspect of those days is the photograph of the barnyard on the Eslinger family farm in East Pennsboro Township as it looked around the turn of the century.

When Harrisburg was still a borough, this is how it may have looked at Calder's stagecoach depot on Market Square. A stage has arrived at the terminal point and horses, passengers, and baggage are exchanged.

heartburnings among members of to-day's school board.

From 1849 into the 1860s the Harrisburg Female Seminary flourished on Locust Street on the site of the present Telegraph Building, a location which in 1858 was noted as "the most quiet and retired portion of the town." James W. Weir, John C. Kunkel, J. Adams Fisher, Daniel D. Boas, James R. Jones, William M. Kerr, and George H. Small were prominent citizens who served the Seminary as trustees.

Another women's school—Pennsylvania Female College—was incorporated in 1853 and was housed in the Harris Mansion. It had a comparatively brief existence and never a large enrollment; in 1858 its student body numbered only eight-four.

The Harrisburg Academy (now moved to the West Shore) existed as early as 1809. In its long and honorable history the Academy graduated hun-

Grave markers in various sizes, shapes, and materials have been around since time immemorial, and John Beatty, who lived at 19 South Fourth Street, for some years was in that business. Marble was quite popular and much less expensive in those days; so Mr. Beatty specialized in that material, many samples of which still may be seen in local cemeteries.

Church on South Second Street December 12, 1854. (The church, built in 1842 and burned in 1858, stood at the intersection of South Second Street and Cherry Alley, and was next door to the governor's mansion, last occupied by Governor Andrew G. Curtin.) A week later they adopted a constitution and bylaws and elected Judge John W. Simonton president.

The first regular meeting place of the Harrisburg YMCA was a rented room in the Kelker Building at 118-120 Market Street, at the northeast corner of that street and River Alley. It was secured

A venerable travelers' rest was the old Mansion House at the corner of Second and Mulberry streets. History notes that General Lafayette stopped here overnight during his visit to the United States in 1825. Originally it was the United States Hotel, later Small's Hotel (1839-41). It was torn down shortly after the above picture was taken in the early 1900s to make way for the Second Street railroad underpass.

Note the steps leading to the front entrance of the Colonel Kieffer residence next door, indicating the original street level before construction of the Cumberland Valley Railroad grade in 1837. The crossing watchman's shelter and the crossing gates can be seen in the foreground.

The John W. Reily family starts for Harrisburg on an early spring day in the early 1900's, via the River Road (Rt. 22). Their mode of transportation from the 1400-acre Reily Farm at Fort Hunter is this splendid horse-drawn coach driven by Isaac Turns, the family's "right-hand man."

A graduate of the Harrisburg Academy, Reily was active in the iron industry for 35 years before taking up farming. He built and operated the Lucknow Forge, later selling it to the Pennsylvania Railroad when that company expanded its yards. The site is now occupied by a rail welding plant. Married to Helen M. Boas, daughter of Daniel and Margaret (Bates) Boas in 1887, Mr. Reily and his wife were active in social, civic and religious circles until his death in 1927.

The above "candid camera" picture from the past was taken by the late William Shatto, from the bedroom window of his home and was made available by his son, John L. Shatto, of West Fairview.

dreds of young Harrisburgers whose names became prominent in the commercial, legal, political, and cultural life of the community. Its building stood on Front Street, some distance above South.

Harrisburg owes much to the good influence of the YMCA. Founded on June 6, 1844, in London by George Williams, the Young Men's Christian Association spread quickly to the United States. Harrisburg organized one of the first eight Associations in the country at a meeting of leading citizens held in the lecture room of the English Presbyterian

through the interest of Rudolph Kelker, who later became the ''Y'' 's second president and remained active in the ''Y'' for forty years.

The Harrisburg YMCA had three homes prior to 1877. The first was the Kelker Building, mentioned above; the second, two rooms of the Wyeth Building (later the Caplan Building) at 3 North Market Square; the third, three rooms at 26 North Third Street, later occupied by the Schleisner Store.

Even the last headquarters, however, was not large enough to accommodate the increasing ''Y'' activities, and a successful financial campaign was launched in early 1877, led by General James A. Beaver (later governor) and the Association's president, Judge Samuel J. M. McCarrell. The old Pennsylvania Hotel at Second and Locust streets was bought on April 18, 1877, and occupied in August. This purchase of the first

''Y''-owned home was made possible through the generous contribution of James McCormick, one of the organizers in 1854. A gymnasium and hall were added the following year.

In 1902 the ''Y'' moved to temporary quarters at 228 North Third Street while its old building was removed and a new one constructed on the same site as the old. The ''Y'' occupied the new building in 1903. It abandoned this building in 1933 and sold it in 1934. After many years as an office building, this structure was torn down in 1974.

In 1933, undaunted by the stock market crash and the Great Depression that followed, the ''Y'' carried out a building campaign that resulted in a new Central ''Y'' at Front and North streets and expansion of the ''Y'' summer camp, Camp Shikellimy. A point of interest in this connection is that the Central ''Y'' was erected on the site of the 1850 Pel-

The Dauphin Building in Market Square today could be called ''a house of many names.'' The brick building, in much different form, first replaced a log hostelry named the Union Hotel, then the Washington Hotel, followed by the Jones House, where Lincoln stayed overnight. With another change of owners it was named the Leland Hotel, and this is how it looked in 1887. Finally it became the Commonwealth Hotel, which many older residents remember. Since 1916, when it became the property of the Dauphin Trust Company, its Grecian architecture has graced Market Street, and it has been used as an office building.

Note the old market shed in the Square and the pile of watermelons under shelter on that rainy day in 1887 when the above photograph was taken.

gram & Meyer cotton mill, later a silk mill.

Mention should also be made of the Forster Street "Y." This branch was organized in 1919. It first occupied a room on the first floor of a building at Briggs and Cowden streets (Cowden Street has since been obliterated by the expansion of the Capitol complex). From 1920 to 1928 it made its home at 644 Broad Street. The third home of the Forster Street "Y" was in the Holy Cross Parish Hall at Forster and Cowden streets. In 1931 it occupied a new building at 614-624 Forster Street. The Forster Street Branch was replaced by the Camp Curtin Branch of the "Y", occupying a new building at Sixth and Woodbine streets, in 1966. Shortly after the Camp Curtin "Y" opened, the Forster Street building was removed in the Capitol area expansion.

The foregoing has been mainly a historic detailing of the YMCA's various homes; to treat of its activities in the community and the men who fostered them would require a book in itself. A random sampling of the civic leaders would include the names of Robert A. Enders, Arthur D. Bacon, George R. Bailey, John E. Fox, Roy H. Stetler, Frank J. Wallis, Arthur H. Hull, E. Z. Wallower, Frank B. Wickersham, Mark T. Milnor, Charles A. Kunkel, Adam K. Fahnestock, John Y. Boyd, John Fox Weiss—and these are only a few. For the history of Harrisburg's YMCA up to 1954—its centennial year—Hubert C. Eicher's *A Century of Service* is recommended.

Of all wars involving the U.S.A., that with Mexico (1846-1848) touched Harrisburg least closely. Though several companies of militia represented the city, only one appears to have been accepted for service—the Cameron Guards. They marched to Pittsburgh in the dead of winter to be mustered in and were sent from there to New Orleans. On March 29, 1847, they arrived at Vera

The Central Iron & Steel Company and its associated Chesapeake Nail Works evolved from an iron furnace established by James McCormick in the 1850s in south Harrisburg. Within thirty years it had expanded into the extensive plant shown in this steel engraving. Note the rows of "company houses" in close proximity to the mills. Some of these buildings survived until the 1950s, when the industry closed down forever.

Cruz. The Guards fought at Chapultepec, where their captain, Edward C. Williams, scored another first for Harrisburg by raising the first American flag over the captured citadel. That flag, which was also raised over Mexico City, was later placed in the State Museum. At the close of the war Harrisburg welcomed back the thirty-two survivors out of the ninety-seven listed on the Guard's roll. A monument in Capitol Park commemorates Pennsylvania's part in the war.

In its years as a borough Harrisburg grew by the proverbial "leaps and bounds," due in large measure to its position as a "crossroads of the East." By the time it was incorporated as a city (1860) the population had increased from 1472 in 1800 to well over 16,000. Records for 1858 show 22 dry-goods stores, 44 grocery stores, 104 other mercantile establishments, 5 breweries, and at least 52 eating houses and taverns. Large-scale manufacturing gave employment to hundreds of citizens: the Bay and Jennings iron foundries, Harrisburg Car Factory, Keystone Iron Works, the rolling mills of Pratt & Son and Bailey & Brother, the Porter and McCormick furnaces, and the Pelgram & Meyer Cotton Mill.

Before taking up the story of Harrisburg from the time it became a city, it would be well to consider four of the reasons for its growth and importance. To be covered in the next chapter are lumbering, the Pennsylvania Canal, the railroads, and highways.

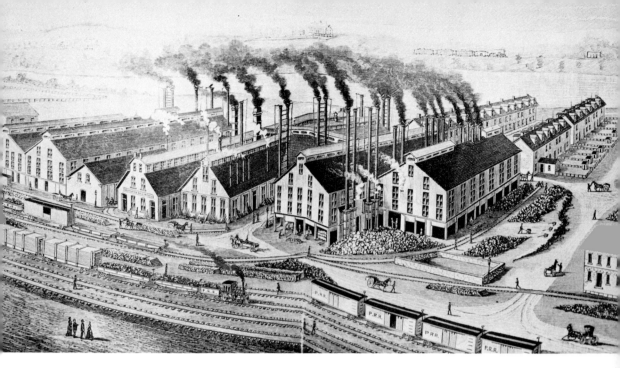

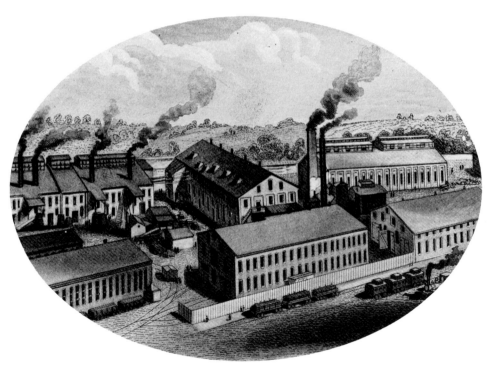

A forerunner of the present Harrisburg Steel Company was the Harrisburg Car Works, depicted here. It was established in 1853 through the efforts of David Fleming. The original wooden buildings of the company were completely destroyed by fire in 1872. Rebuilt immediately under the supervision of William D. Hildrup, Sr., the industry expanded to include the construction of an early type railroad refrigerator car. A banking house failure put the company out of business in 1890.

Hildrup, assisted by David E. Tracy and J. Hervey Patton, then organized the Harrisburg Pipe & Pipe Bending Company on a financial shoestring the next year. Their venture succeeded and led to the creation of one of the city's present-day leading industries, the Harrisburg Steel Company.

In the earliest pioneer days in Pennsylvania the two primary industries in every community were the gristmill and the sawmill. The gristmill ground the farmers' grain for food and what little they had left over to sell; the sawmill prepared the lumber for building barns and houses. Harrisburg had its share of both, run by water power before the era of steam.

LUMBERING

Pennsylvania—Penn's Woods—was well named. When settlers first moved into the lands west of the Delaware, they entered an area that was largely forest, broken here and there by small, natural meadows and patches of relatively open ground. Every farmer had to clear the trees from a large portion of his land,

In the days of log rafts on the river sawmills dotted the shores in the Harrisburg area. One of these was located just opposite the city on the West Shore between the Market and Walnut Street bridges. The mill office was located in the small frame building next to the backyard fence of the toll collector's house. In the background is the Bridgeport Hotel, operated by John Bretz. The inn's large whitewashed barn parallels the tracks of the Harrisburg & Mechanicsburg Electric Railway. The buildings were torn down in 1902 to make way for the Pennsylvania Railroad low grade line.

Chapter 7

Lumbering, Canals, Railroads, and Highways

either by burning or cutting. By the early 1800s southeastern Pennsylvania could no longer furnish enough timber locally to supply the constantly increasing demand for construction lumber in its towns.

However, in one vast area of the state—the present counties of Cameron, Clarion, Clearfield, Forest, Lycoming, Potter, and Tioga—the splendid forests

of white pine and hemlock had been practically untouched. In those days before the railroads reached up into the northern counties, overland transportation of lumber to southern Pennsylvania by wagons would have been impossibly expensive. But there was the river, a broad highway linking the two sections.

A look at a topographical map of the state confirms why the lumber industry became a major influence in the early prosperity of Harrisburg. The Susquehanna and its branches drain not only a huge 21,000 square miles of the state, but in addition some 6000 square miles in New York State. This compares with the total drainage of the Ohio River of not quite 23,000 and of the Delaware of 10,000. Obviously the Susquehanna, with its headwaters in the finest pine and hemlock forests in the state, was not only the most logical but also the best route for moving lumber cheaply.

So as early as 1807 lumbermen began to float timber down the river in rafts. This rafting enjoyed its heyday in the years between 1833 and 1840, when each year from 2000 to 2500 huge rafts came down the river in the spring and fall. About half of these were broken up and sold at Harrisburg, Middletown, and Marietta. The remainder went on down the river to tidewater.

These rafts were tremendous affairs. Made up of huge logs of virgin pine and hemlock 25 to 30 feet long, the rafts themselves were from 150 up to 300 feet in length. The logs were lashed side by side to give the raft a width, usually, of about twenty-four feet. If wider than that, a raft could not pass through the many chutes (places between rocks) in

the river. Ordinarily four or five men constituted a raft crew as far as Marietta; from there to tidewater nine or ten crewmen were needed because of the increased hazards of steering between the protruding rocks in the river. Long, heavy sweep-oars steered the cumbersome craft. In dangerous sections of the river the rafts were tied up at night; if the "sailing" was smooth, rafts could "run" all night. Crew members not on duty then slept or prepared meals in shacks on the rafts.

Raftsmen were a hardy breed, skilled in their specialized work. They were to the East what the cowboys were to the West. Hard-working, hard-drinking, hard-living, they were the men who made the Pennsylvania Bucktails famous in the Civil War with their expert sharpshooting. Their whole life was timber—cutting it in the winter and summer and rafting it to market on the waters of the spring thaw, the "June freshet," and the autumn rains. When modern lumbering methods and rail transport gradually replaced them, like the old soldiers of the song they did not die, they simply faded away. With their going a romantic era ended in Pennsylvania history.

Log rafts on the river at Harrisburg were already becoming a rarity as the nineteenth century drew to a close. The photographer, apparently forewarned, took the above picture from the Walnut Street Bridge as the raft with two crewmen at the sweeps steered a course between the piers of the old covered bridge at Market Street.

Harrisburg's first steam-operated planing mill was conveniently located along the Pennsylvania Canal, adjacent to the original Penn Lock in south Harrisburg. The sketch shows a load of lumber just leaving the loading dock. John B. Simon was the proprietor of the mill at the time (1870).

But in their day the raftsmen made things lively in the riverside towns. During the late winter and early spring they floated logs down creeks and sluices to the river booms—dams made by chaining logs across the upper reaches of the river. Here the rafts were put together to await the high water when the booms would be opened and the rafts started on their long journey south. Once the raftsmen were on their way they were seldom in dry clothes until the end of the run. As the rafts passed through rough water or rapids the men were constantly drenched with the spray spouting up between the logs. To offset the resulting chills, whiskey in large quantities was the most obvious—and pleasantest!—remedy. Every river town had its waterside saloons and taverns to provide this necessity. If a raft was running the river on a good night instead of tying up until morning, tavern keepers sent out boats loaded with liquid antidote to meet the rafts and fortify their chill-threatened operators.

Harrisburg had its full share in this. Her "Hardscrabble" section along the riverfront catered to the lumbermen. When rafts tied up or were moored for sale and dismantling, brawling was a nightly occurrence; "drunken raftsmen" was a common epithet on the tongues of the staid, workaday citizens.

John Yingst, merchant at 1200 North Front Street in the old "Hardscrabble" section of the city, sold assorted household furnishings of the day, in addition to ice cream in the parlor of his home next door.

"Hardscrabble" is said to have derived its name from an early stone home which bore the title "Hart's Rabble." It grew up along the river in rafting days and was where the crews tied up for rest, recreation and refreshment—mostly refreshment and recreation of a nature that provided that part of the city with its unusual name. The neighborhood vanished about 1922 to make way for the city's sunken gardens.

The town then paralleled in smaller measure a western cow town at the end of a cattle drive. But also, as in the cow town's situation, the raftsmen brought a measure of prosperity. Like the cowboys, they spent lavishly for food and drink and they brought a much-needed product which put money in the coffers of sawmill owners, carpenters, and storekeepers.

Rafting flourished for almost two generations; after the great rafting year of 1873 there was a gradual decline as more and more sawmills in the northern counties began to convert logs into lumber and ship the boards by canal and rail. But, as late as 1889, the great flood that year swept thousands of boom logs (logs held in the upper river booms and not yet made up into rafts) down the Susquehanna. They covered the islands opposite Harrisburg and so threatened the Cumberland Valley Railroad bridge that long trains of heavily laden cars were run onto the bridge to weight it down and hold it in place against the battering of the heavy, flood-driven timbers.

In March, 1938, a group of the nostalgia-minded organized in Clearfield County, on the West Branch of the Susquehanna, what they called "The Last Raft." A symbolic raft was constructed and started down the river, manned by a large crew of enthusiastic amateurs. They ran by day, tying up at night. Harrisburg papers faithfully reported their progress. But the raft never reached Harrisburg. Disaster overtook it near Fort Hunter, where the raft broke up, a crew member was drowned, and the adventure was sadly abandoned.

THE CANAL ERA

Even before the 1800s the idea of canals for transport had begun to occupy men's minds in America. The rapid expansion westward brought with it the problem of supplying the settlements that sprang up far inland and relatively remote from good roads and natural waterways. The pack-saddle caravans and wagon trains of the time were no

The Flood of 1889, sparked by the same deluge that caused the disaster at Johnstown, piled logs and other debris against the steel framework of the Cumberland Valley Railroad bridge at Harrisburg. The view is from the east shore looking towards Bridgeport and Ft. Washington. The Camelback Bridge can be seen at the extreme right.

Ladies were permitted to ride on the mules that pulled canal boats on Sunday afternoon excursions along the waterways, a fun thing in those days. No such monkey business for the lady seated under an umbrella in the bow of the boat, however, despite the obvious male approval.

answer to the demand for transport. Usually the roads were simply broad paths hacked through timberland, unmetalled trails that in rainy weather became muddy furrows that could bog a heavily laden horse fetlock-deep or a wagon axle-deep.

In that age before railroads men turned to waterways as the only alternative. Natural watercourses to inland settlements had one great drawback: Rivers flow *to* the sea, not *away* from it to where the settlements were, and the labor, difficulty, and expense of towing a barge or boat upstream made that expedient unfeasible. But water was still the answer; if rivers would not serve, men could make their own waterways. In a word, canals.

The story of canals goes back into the earliest history of mankind. But most of the canals in America owed their exist-

ence to one comparatively modern device: the hydraulic lock, devised in Italy in 1481. European, Asian, and Egyptian canals, traversing usually level ground, used no locking system to raise or lower boats where the ground level changed. They were simply dug around the obstructing elevation, or goods were transported overland to a continuation of the canal. Eastern America, with its general slope to the Atlantic, and its ranges of hills and mountains, had to use locks if the canals were to have any practical advantage.

Canals are of two classes: large (or ship) canals, and small (or barge) canals. It was the latter that concerned the United States in the feverish days of canal construction in the first third of the nineteenth century. While it is not intended to present a treatise on canals—or rafting or railroads—the fact that

Harrisburg has been at different times an important center in each mode of transportation makes a more than cursory comment on each desirable.

So Harrisburg and its part in the Pennsylvania Canal is the theme. It is interesting to know how the two came together. The account begins as early as 1791, when John Harris' town was—figuratively—in its babyhood. In that year Robert Morris' Society for Promoting the Improvement of Roads and Inland Navigation suggested a canal route beginning at the Schuylkill River on the eastern boundary of the state and crossing Pennsylvania to Pittsburgh at the western end, figuring a distance of 426 miles. As Morris envisioned it optimistically, the canal would use streams and rivers, with a minimum of actual canal construction.

The Morris suggestion was made about the same time as work began on a Schuylkill-Susquehanna canal, which had been planned as early as 1762. Construction was slow at first—only four miles were completed by 1794—but by 1827 the canal was finished and named Union Canal.

What gave the final impetus to the Pennsylvania Canal proposal was New York's triumphant completion of her Erie Canal. On March 27, 1824, the Pennsylvania Legislature authorized the governor to appoint a commission to examine possible canal routes from Harrisburg to Pittsburgh. Actually, the canal was to begin at the Schuylkill; the plan was to absorb the already existing, privately owned Union Canal as a branch line, and utilize a soon-to-be-constructed horse-powered Philadelphia-Columbia Railway to link the Schuylkill and the Susquehanna. The commission, consisting of James Clark, Colonel Jacob Holgate, and Charles Treziyulney, duly made their route exploration and returned a majority favorable report. Treziyulney, the dissenter, felt that the mountainous nature of the western half of the route presented too many obstacles to make the canal practicable.

This objection, plus a growing belief in the efficiency of a railroad from Philadelphia to Pittsburgh, led to the appointment of another commission, this one to study the possibility of a rail line instead of a canal. This was in 1825, and although this second commission favored the railroad, they were a little ahead of their time: people were not yet ready for steam locomotion; moreover, the universal "canal fever" was still high.

The whole problem was definitely settled when on February 25, 1826, Governor Shulze signed an act providing for the construction of a canal "at the expense of the State . . . to be styled the Pennsylvania Canal." Construction progressed comparatively rapidly; by 1834 the system was in operation. It included the remarkable Allegheny Por-

Take the Pioneer Fast Line! Only three and one-half days from Philadelphia to Pittsburgh. What is more, one could board a river boat there and travel along with the U.S. Mail to Louisville, Kentucky, if one desired. This 1837 poster proclaimed the advantages of rail and canal travel over that offered by the stagecoaches of that day.

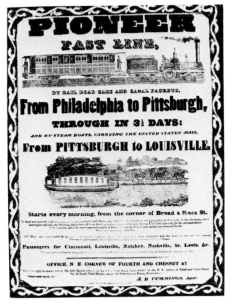

tage Railway for carrying the canalboats and barges over the mountain by the use of inclined planes.

Statistics are often dull, but those relating to the canal, which once meant so much to the growth and prosperity of Harrisburg, should be interesting. The 394.25-mile stretch of the Pennsylvania Canal system was in five sections, the first and fourth of which have already been named, the Philadelphia-Columbia and the Allegheny Portage railways.

Of the remaining three sections, which constituted the canal proper, the second was the Eastern Division, from the junction with the Union Canal at Middletown north twenty-four miles along the east shore of the river to the mouth of the Juniata. The third was the Juniata Division; here the canal crossed the Susquehanna at Duncan's Island, thence on an aqueduct over the Juniata to follow the south bank of that river to Hollidaysburg. The fifth division was the Western, from Laurel Hill to Pittsburgh.

This sketch-history of Harrisburg is concerned only with the second section, the Eastern Division. It was in Harrisburg that the first lock of the Eastern Division was constructed. On July 4, 1826, Governor Shulze initiated the work by turning the first spadeful of earth for Lock No. 6 (the Penn Lock) at the foot of Walnut Street. On March 14 the following year "a great concourse of people" including members of the Legislature, the town burgess, and the Council attended the laying of the cornerstone in Masonic form by the governor. It was a historic event for Harrisburg, and a historic date; it marked the beginning of Harrisburg's rise as a transportation center, since the canal was the immediate forerunner of the Pennsylvania Railroad system.

Almost exactly a year later, on March 20, 1828, water was let into the canal at McAllister's Mill, near Rockville, and then a new era began for Harrisburg with the completion of the Pennsylvania Canal in 1834. Going "down to the lock" to watch the canalboats pass became a popular form of entertainment, just as later one went to the station or a viewpoint along the tracks to watch the trains go by.

What were they like, the canal and the locks, and the vessels and their crews that passed through them? The canal: it was simply a big ditch, forty feet wide at the waterline when full, twenty-eight feet at the bottom, and with a minimum depth of four feet. The water was held in by the normal banks of the ditch, except where very porous soil required "puddling." This was the coating of the bed and sides of the canal with a special clay. A two- to three-foot thickness of this "puddle" was sometimes necessary to make the canal watertight. The ground was leveled on one side of the canal to provide a towpath for the horses or mules which pulled the barges.

The locks—there were thirteen of them in the Eastern Division—were the most interesting feature of the canal. They were uniformly ninety feet long by seventeen feet wide, and had an average lift of about eight feet. The walls were of carefully fitted stone blocks, usually quarried locally, and so well constructed that many exist today in good condition despite the ravages of time and neglect since the canal was abandoned three-quarters of a century ago, in 1901. The lock chamber had a pair of solid oak gates at each end, opening upstream against the slight current. When a barge came up, the upper gates were closed and the lower gates' sluices— small, windowlike openings at the bottom of the gates—were opened to allow water to run out until canal and lock levels equalized. The lower gates were then opened, the barge entered the lock, the gates and sluices were closed, and sluices in the upper gates were opened to fill the lock and raise the barge to the higher level. Each lock had a lock-

Visiting author Charles Dickens did not think much of travel by canal packet boat, the passenger craft of yesteryear. The discomforts suffered by travelers in those days were graphically described in his account of a trip between Harrisburg and Pittsburgh in the 1840s. Shown here is an artist's concept of this mode of transportation.

The chief engineer of the Pennsylvania Canal, Eastern Division, had his private yacht, just as railroad officials in later years had their own mobile office cars. That official, Thomas T. Wierman, had his headquarters at 504½ Market Street, Harrisburg, but much of the time used the steamboat pictured below to keep in touch with canal operations and employees. His home during those years was 116 Pine Street

Employees of the Cowden & Wilcox Pottery pose for a photograph with F. H. Cowden (front center), their boss. Front row, l. to r., James Dunn, unknown, Cowden, and Harry Bowman. Rear, l. to r., unknown, Irvin Wenrick, Arthur Wert, Bill Garner, unknown, Tom Phybie, and John Page.

tender to operate the heavy beams and bars controlling the massive gates and their sluices. The canal commissioners provided him—and his family, if he was married—with a rent-free house close to the lock, since he had to be on call twenty-four hours a day, seven days a week.

The canal and its locks, however, were obviously only means to one end: transportation of goods and passengers.

Canalboats, or barges, were blunt-ended, massive-looking vessels, flat on top and bottom. To make a homely comparison, they resembled in a general way giant shoeboxes with rounded corners. To fit into the locks their width was restricted to less than fifteen feet; their length was usually considerably less than the ninety-foot lock length. They were of two types: packet, or passenger boat; and freight barge. The twenty- to thirty-ton boats moved at an average two-mile-an-hour pace by horse- or mule-power.

The towline varied in length according to conditions along the canal, but the usual line was a "sixty-five-yarder." This allowed for passing. Since there was but one towpath, when two boats met the rule was for each boat to turn out to its right. The boat with its tow-horse pulling to its left swung to the opposite side of the canal, and the horse moved away from the channel and towpath and stopped, allowing the towline to sink in the water; the other boat was drawn over the submerged line. When a boat (usually a packet) overtook another (usually a freighter), the overtaken boat swung wide to the left and dropped its line by stopping—if its captain was in a cooperative mood!

And this brings up the canallers, or

"canawlers" as they called themselves. Like the raftsmen discussed earlier, they were a very special breed, hardy, independent, pugnacious, and profane. Many were Irishmen who had helped dig the canal. Too restless to settle down, they took to canalling. On the freight barges that ran only in daytime a crew of three was the usual custom: the steersman who manned the big rudder's long tiller, guiding the boat against the inward pull of the towline; the captain, who gave the orders, cooked the meals, and relieved the steersman; and the driver, whose job it was to keep the perpetually tired tow-horse (or skittish mule) in motion. He walked beside the animal, on the landward side to avoid accident if the towline was suddenly snapped taut. One of his ex-officio duties was to keep an eye peeled for stray chickens or cornfields near the canal; such delicacies were welcome additions to the regular fare of bacon, beans, bread, and coffee.

One horse usually constituted the motive power. If two were used for an extra-heavy cargo or for speed, they were hitched in tandem. If a "one-horse" barge captain could afford two animals to spell each other, the idle one had a stall on the boat. More often than not, there was only one horse. Though it was well-fed, the animal never got enough rest and was always half-wornout. Query: Could this account for the expression "one-horse town"?

Passenger-carrying packets, which often traveled day and night, boasted larger crews (for relief steersmen and drivers) and a cook, a steward, and sometimes—on the plush packets— even a chambermaid—!

Wharves for loading or unloading freight or passengers were built on the canal side opposite the towpath so as not to interfere with traffic. At towns or other convenient intervals harbors were made by widening the canal. Here boats and barges could lay up overnight or on

Wister's Iron Furnace was located along the canal just south of the foot of Third Street. Built in 1867, it was acquired and torn down in the 1880s by the Philadelphia & Reading Railway to make way for the approach to that railroad's first bridge across the river.

Sunday, and the canallers could take off for a riotous night on the town.

Two other features of the canal should be mentioned, the bridges and the aqueducts. Bridges were numerous, since the canal's right-of-way often bisected a farm and the farmer had to have a means of getting from one of his fields to another. The bridges usually provided very little clearance; one of the steersman's duties was to call out "Low bridge!" at the approach to one as a caution to crew members or passengers taking in the scenery from the top of the cabin. Bumped heads, a ducking in the canal, or even a cracked skull could result from failure to heed the warning.

Aqueducts were, in effect, huge troughs over streams or low ground. They were often covered and local youngsters had the novel fun in summer of bathing in the shade, high in the air. Where the aqueduct was not covered, it furnished countryfolk with the jaw-dropping marvel of boats sailing in the sky above them.

Also worthy of at least brief mention are the weigh-locks. Here the toll collectors would weigh an empty vessel by letting all water out of the lock until the boat rested on scales. Then by adding "kentledge" (pig iron bars of known weight) to the boat when it was again floated, the collector could mark the hull with brass nails at the waterline at two-ton intervals for future determination of the toll. One of these weigh-locks was at Harrisburg.

At the height of the canal craze just about every town wanted a waterway in the belief that a canal would automatically bring prosperity and growth. But

The second railroad crossing of the Susquehanna in this area was made at Rockville, seven miles north of the city, in 1849. The first was that of the Cumberland Valley Railroad connecting Harrisburg with the West Shore ten years prior to that date. The Pennsylvania Railroad structure pictured here was 3680 feet long, consisting of 23 spans, each 160 feet in length. The photograph, probably taken in the 1860s, includes the tracks of the Northern Central Railway (at bottom of photo, partially obscured by the building in the foreground). The Northern Central Railway had built north from Bridgeport (Lemoyne) on the west bank of the river in 1857, and constructed its own river crossing a short distance upstream from the Pennsylvania Railroad bridge.

Pride of the Pennsylvania Railroad's great fleet of passenger trains in the 1890s was the Pennsylvania Limited, later to become the famous Broadway Limited. Shortly after its inaugural run a railroad photographer induced it to halt momentarily at the west end of the Rockville Bridge for this photo.

many towns soon found that the canal was not an unmixed blessing. The labor gangs who dug the canal were a rough-and-ready lot. At night and on Sundays their drinking, fighting, and carousing made life a nightmare in the staid towns through which the canal passed.

Then with the completion of the canal and the letting in of water, the channel soon became something approaching an open sewer. A dumping ground for garbage from the canalboats and a convenient place for surreptitious disposal of the waste of farms and towns—even dead animals—its odor in summer was something short of attar of roses. There was always the danger of small children falling in and drowning. And there were the canallers with their drinking and swearing to shock and offend the stay-at-home townsmen who naturally looked with suspicion at folk without settled habitation. Winter brought a respite—but no revenue—with the barges either frozen in or stranded in drained sections, and the canallers gone for a time. Then there was skating on the

ice in the undrained parts of the canal, and the garbage smell faded to an unpleasant memory.

Much of this account applied to Harrisburg as an important canal town. Whatever its shortcomings and drawbacks, the Pennsylvania Canal did bring prosperity to the town. It carried out manufactured goods and brought in necessities and luxuries. Travelers and canallers spent money in the city to the profit of local merchants.

But almost from the start the canal's days were numbered. Railroads, with their all-year operation, cheaper line construction, and immensely greater capacity and speed, began to supersede canals, often laying their lines on the old canal beds. In Harrisburg it is difficult for any but canal buffs to trace the old canal line. It paralleled the river approximately between Seventh and Ninth streets through the town, and then swung west to run northward beside the river. Filled in and built over, all but a few traces have vanished. It is known, for example, that the canal passed be-

The double-lift lock at the intersection of Walnut Street and the canal was constructed in 1857-58, replacing the original Penn Lock, located a bit south of Market Street to permit the construction of the first Philadelphia & Reading passenger station here.

A canal boat passes beneath an overpass near Herr Street, and approaches a building of the Cowden & Wilcox Pottery on a summer day in the 1880s. On the opposite side of the waterway are buildings of the Harrisburg Car Works. The small brick structure opposite the end of the bridge stands today in the yard of the J. C. Budding Company building supplies complex on the north side of Herr Street.

tween the Pennsylvania Station and the old Philadelphia & Reading Railroad Station (the latter was at the site of the present-day main post office), but time and change have obliterated it. At Steelton a part of the canal serves as a channel for water for the mills. Since this Eastern Division of the canal was the last to be abandoned (in 1901), one can still find the canal line and some of its locks north and south of Harrisburg.

The era stirred with change—a change away from the flesh-and-blood horse of the stage line and the canalboat to the "iron horse" of the railroad. In point of fact, there was really no abrupt change from the canal to the railroad; rather, it was a blending and a slow transition that brought its corresponding change in the life of Harrisburg. In the heyday of the canal Harrisburg had proudly considered itself a bustling commercial community; with the coming of the railroad it found itself hustling, almost against its will. Not always happily, citizens accepted the smoke and noise of the train, the dust stirred up by the hurrying drays with their loads of freight from those trains, and the generally heightened tempo of life as the price to be paid for progress.

Indian trails, pioneer roads, stage roads, and the canal had already made Harrisburg a junction point for traffic to and from the four points of the compass. It naturally followed that the city should become an important rail center, perhaps the most important in the East. But in this little history one can only sketch briefly the story of how that came about.

The Stream Cars Arrive

On September 16, 1836, a crowd of frock-coated, tall-hatted men and fashionably bonnetted women gathered at the site of the present Penn-Central Railroad Station to witness a novel sight. It was the arrival of the first train

P. R. R. PASSENGER & FREIGHT SCHEDULE
ON AND AFTER MONDAY, OCTOBER 14, 1850.

LEAVE WESTWARD							STATIONS	Miles	LEAVE EASTWARD					
Columbia Branch	Local Freight	Through Freight	Slow Passenger	Passenger	Fast Passenger	Numbers			Fast Passenger	Passenger	Slow Passenger	Through Freight	Local Freight	Columbia Branch
P.M.	M.	A.M.	P.M.	A.M.	A.M.				P.M.	A.M.	P.M.	P.M.	A.M.	P.M.
6 30	12 00						Columbia						11 30	6 00
		6 30	9 30	2 30	11 30	2	Dillerville	110	6 36	8 30	8 30	6 00		
		7 54			12 05	6	Mount Joy	64	6 03	7 54				
			10 45	3 30	12 28	7	Elizabeth T.	87	5 42	7 34	7 15	4 00		
	12 56	10 00	A. M.		12 56	9	Middle T.	99	5 12	7 01			10 00	5 12
8 30		10 50	6 30	4 45	*2 00	11	Harrisburg	104	4 41	6 30	6 00	2 00		9 30
			7 22	5 15	2 28	13	Cove	40		5 15	4 37			
			7 42		2 39	14	Duncannon	84	3 49	5 00	4 17			
			8 24		3 03	16	Bailey's	46	3 27	4 35	3 37			
			8 47		3 17	17	Newport	52	3 17		3 17			
			9 13	6 18	3 35	18	Millers T.	162	3 00	4 00	2 48			
			10 33	7 25	4 15	22	Mifflin	118	2 20	3 00	*1 36			
		*12 12	7 51		4 46	23	Lewistown	119	*1 52	2 17	12 12			
		1 04	8 20	5 17	25		M'Veytown	130	1 04	1 30	11 18			
			2 09		5 49	27	Mt. Union	140		12 41	10 20			
			2 42		6 06	29	Mill Creek	50		12 16	9 52			
			3 07	9 27	6 22	30	Huntingdon	66	12 07	11 57	9 27			
			3 40		6 39	31	Petersburg	58		11 29	8 40			
			4 09	10 03	6 56	32	Spruce Creek	70	11 38	11 07	8 20			
			4 41	10 24	7 24	33	Tyrone	65	11 10	10 39	7 45			
			5 12	10 47		34	Fostoria	82	10 47		7 13			
			5 54	11 15	7 56	35	Altoona	64	10 22	9 44	6 32			
			†6 20	11 35	†8 15	36	Intersection		10 00	9 20	6 00			
	P.M.	A.M.	P.M.						A.M. P.M. M. A.M.					

The passing places are indicated by the large type.

Eastward trains have preference of road. They are not to wait for Westward trains, but run with great caution, if they are not found at the passing places. In all cases of detention, conform to rule 4 for passenger engine men.

If passenger trains are detained, freight trains must wait for them until they have passed, unless written orders to the contrary have been received from a reliable source.

Ballast, express, and all extra trains must give notice of the field of their operations, and make constant use of the caution and danger signals. Conductors and engineers are both held responsible for running curves, and in case of accident, both will be liable to dismissal, if any precaution has been omitted, even though the rules should not have provided for the case.

The maximum speed of past passenger trains is 2 minutes to a mile; for slow passenger trains 2½ minutes, and for freight, 3 minutes, to be reduced when not consistent with safety.

Compare time daily with office clock at Harrisburg. Never leave a station until the time is fully up. Pass bridges at 6 minutes to a mile. Run slowly around curves. Report slides, accidents, detentions, defects in track, &c., to the Superintendent, with the number of the nearest mile post. Observe whistling posts and caution boards.

Freight and irregular trains must keep out of the way of passengers 20 minutes when running in opposite directions, and ten minutes when running in the same direction.

If the cars of the Portage and Cumberland Valley roads are in sight when the time arrives for leaving, wait for them. Wait for Westward passenger trains at Dillerville until 2 P. M. and 6 A. M.

If the Columbia train is not in, wait at Middletown ten minutes; the Columbia train will, in that case, run to Harrisburg, if it can go there, and return before the Eastward train arrives at Middletown.

Agents, watchmen and track repairers must not fail to report engineers who run beyond the maximum speed allowed, or leave any station ahead of time.

Fast trains will stop at Aqueduct and other points where connections are made with other lines; also, at way stations when necessary to discharge through passenger.

Fast passenger trains East will stop for passengers at Duncannon.

*Passengers dine. †Passengers take supper. ‡Passengers take breakfast.

H. HAUPT, Supt.

.Reproduced by J. W. Kauffman

More than a century ago this city was an important terminal point on the railroad which connected with the Pennsylvania Canal at Columbia, and at "Intersection" (Hollidaysburg) to the west. Here is a typical schedule of train service in those days, complete with operating rules, as of October 14, 1850.

in Harrisburg, drawn by a wood-burning locomotive of the new Harrisburg, Portsmouth, Mountjoy & Lancaster Railroad. The name was almost as long as its two-track, thirty-six-mile system. The following year the company built its station here; twelve years later the H.P.M.&L. became a part of the Pennsylvania system, which took over the station, plus all of the motive power and rolling stock.

The Pennsylvania Railroad, eventually to become the nation's greatest rail system, had a stormy and uncertain beginning. As the country emerged from the depression of the early 1840s, a movement got underway to combine the Pennsylvania Canal with a railroad. The

Baltimore & Ohio had in 1828 received state authorization for a line to Pittsburgh and had laid much of the line. In January, 1846, rival bills were introduced in the Legislature: one a repetition of the earlier B&O authorization bill, the other providing for incorporation of the Pennsylvania Central Railroad Company. After considerable political maneuvering the Pennsylvania act was passed by a close vote. It was signed by the governor on April 13, 1846, the official birth date of the mighty Pennsylvania system.

Railroad construction north from Harrisburg promptly ran into its most costly single operation: the mile-long bridge across the Susquehanna at Rockville. It was completed in 1849, replaced in 1877 with an iron truss structure, which in turn gave place to the present stone-arch, four-track bridge in 1902, the longest of its type in the world.

Wherever it was possible, railroads built their lines alongside or directly over the old canals. The reason was, very simply, that the canals had been engineered to maintain an almost level contour. Hence the permanent obliteration of long stretches of the old waterway. In many instances old aqueduct piers served in short bridge construction. So the railroad's gain was the antiquarian's loss.

The station at Harrisburg, originally the H.P.M.&L.'s, was first used in 1849, rebuilt in 1857 and used until 1887, when the first unit of the present building was erected. In 1892 the Pennsylvania opened its Maclay Street Station.

In those hectic days of railroad promotion, with small, independent "feeder"

Remains of Pennsylvania's "big ditch" still were visible from the Mulberry Street Bridge in 1906. A few years later this last vestige was obliterated by expansion of railroad facilities.

While the body of President Abraham Lincoln lay in state in the rotunda of Pennsylvania's capitol on April 21, 1865, the special railroad coach which carried it stood heavily guarded at Harrisburg's second Pennsylvania Railroad passenger station.

lines springing up everywhere, Harrisburg became a meeting place for many. Besides the Pennsylvania Railroad itself, the city was a terminal for the Philadelphia & Reading, the Cumberland Valley, the Northern Central, the Schuylkill & Susquehanna, and the Harrisburg & Potomac. Though they kept their individual names for many years, all became parts of the Pennsylvania Railroad and Philadelphia & Reading systems.

Only one of the above had its own station—the Philadelphia & Reading, at the location mentioned earlier. Their first station, a long frame building built in 1857-58 on the north side of Market Street, was replaced on the opposite side by an imposing stone structure in 1904. The central post office now occupies this site.

Harrisburg's two main passenger depots were busy places up until the late 1920s, when the state inaugurated its highway improvement program. At their peak they accommodated thousands of travelers daily.

The June 1922 *Official Guide of the Railways* lists thirty-two westbound trains arriving on the Philadelphia Division of the Pennsylvania Railroad alone, and thirty-three departing over the Middle Division each twenty-four-hour period. In addition, twelve southbound trains departed daily over the Cumberland Valley Division, and an equal number arrived in this city from Hagerstown, Maryland, and points in the Cumberland Valley. The former Northern Central line from Baltimore and Washington through Harrisburg to Sunbury, Williamsport, Buffalo, and Erie boasted an even dozen passenger trains each way, every day. In addition there were numerous excursion, mail, and express trains.

Just across the tracks the Philadelphia & Reading Railway's smaller, but more

BOILER WORKS OF ROBT. TIPPETT. *HARRISBURG, DAUPHIN CO. PA.*

TIPPETT & JAUSS. FAMILY COAL AND WOOD DEPOT.

Robert Tippett was a local industrialist in the 1870s who relied on railroad transportation, as indicated in these illustrations. He headed a local boiler works (top), and was associated with William Jauss in the operation of a "Family Coal and Wood Depot" (bottom).

attractive, passenger station was the local terminal for sixteen trains arriving from and departing for points in the Lebanon Valley, Reading, Pottsville, Philadelphia, Allentown, and New York City. In addition there were four passenger trains each way between Harrisburg and Gettysburg, and one each way on the Susquehanna & Schuylkill branch.

Harrisburg's central location made it necessary to have facilities for the repair and servicing of equipment and for the distribution of freight. Extensive shops, strategically located many years ago, remain an essential part of today's operations. Freight classification, the sorting and routing of thousands of cars of miscellaneous merchandise and materials, continues to be a big operation here, as it has been ever since the early days of railroading. Marshalling yards just north

of the city's present transportation center, across the river at Enola, and at nearby Rutherford, east of town, have been busy railroad facilities for nigh unto a century, and will be in the foreseeable future as plans for the restructuring of the nation's rail network indicate.

Highways

Purposely reserved in this chapter as the last means of transportation to be discussed are the highways, though actually travel on foot, on horseback, or by wagon came first. But in 150 years— from the beginning of the nineteenth century to the mid-twentieth century— transportation has gone almost full circle from roads, rafting, canals, and railroads, back again to roads.

It is a truism in one sense that the

history of civilization is the history of transportation. Accepting that, one may go back to the narrow Indian trails that intersected at the place where the first John Harris built his trading post and set up his ferry, and where his son later laid out the town that bears his name. It was there and then that the history of civilization began in this part of Pennsylvania.

The Indian trails widened successively for the traveler on horseback, the post rider, and the pack-horse train, and then in turn broadened to the cart-width road—rough and dusty in summer and deep-rutted, muddy, and well-nigh impassable in the wet weather of spring, fall, and winter. The end of the Revolution and the spread of population, with its attendant need for means of communication and channels for the transport of manufactured goods and farm produce, called for new and better highways.

Along with other states, Pennsylvania encouraged private enterprise in road construction; as a result the end of the eighteenth century and the beginning of the nineteenth became the era of the toll road, or turnpike, with the opening of the Lancaster-Philadelphia road in 1794. At intervals along these privately constructed highways, long poles studded with spikes (or ''pikes'') were set up so that they could be pivoted across the road to stop traffic while toll was collected. Once the toll was paid, the pole was swung aside; hence the name ''turnpike,'' which survives today in references to the toll-charging, cross-state Pennsylvania Turnpike. By 1831 there were 220 private companies operating about 2400 miles of toll roads in Pennsylvania, mainly in the southeastern section.

But by the end of the nineteenth century roads were running a poor fourth to the canal, the electric trolley line, and the rapidly proliferating railroad. But also at this time roadbuilding received the ''shot in the arm'' that resulted in giving Pennsylvania and the nation the most elaborate highway system in the world. The invention of the motor car—

Harrisburg has been a center for railroading ever since the formation of the Pennsylvania Railroad in the late 1840s. Stock in the newly formed company sold for $5 a share, as indicated in this reproduction of an 1847 stock receipt issued to Ashbel Green, an early investor.

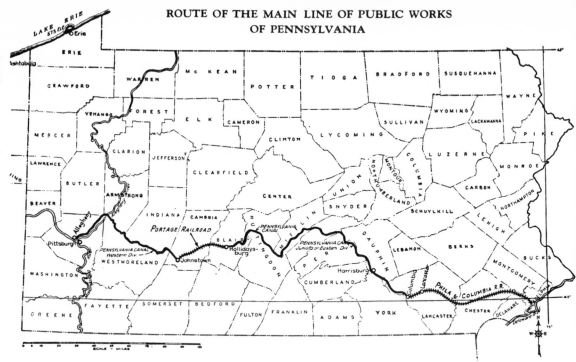

Before the advent of the Pennsylvania Railroad in 1848, the state operated a duplex transportation system of railways and waterways. Harrisburg was prominent, then as now, as a transportation center. On July 4, 1826, the first spadeful of earth was turned in Harrisburg for the construction of the eastern division of the main line of the Pennsylvania Canal between Columbia and Pittsburgh. The map shows the entire length of the Pennsylvania Canal.

One hot July day in 1880 a shifting crew in the Pennsylvania Railroad's Harrisburg freight yards paused long enough in their work to have the above picture taken. Only one of the group has been identified. He is Conductor William B. Steinmetz, the center man of the three leaning against the side of the engine.

The Flood of 1889 did not halt railroad service to and from Harrisburg entirely. Here an eastbound mail train passes a westbound work train just below the Dock Street Bridge. Note the mail clerks leaning out of the doorways. To the left, nearly obscured by haze and smoke, can be seen the outlines of the old canal.

the automobile—not only changed the living habits of people but altered the face of the land as well.

Pennsylvania kept pace with the demands of the times by creating a Highway Department in 1903 (changed to Department of Highways in 1923), granting road improvement aid to counties, townships, and boroughs, and gradually improving road construction from gravel to macadam to concrete for primary highways.

But as late as 1930 the "back roads" of Pennsylvania were still dirt-surfaced, dust-choked in dry weather and quagmires in wet. Gifford Pinchot, running for his second term as governor in 1930, promised if elected to "get the farmers out of the mud." He kept that promise. The state took over some 20,000 miles of rural roads and built the ten- to sixteen-foot-wide "Pinchot roads" for which Pennsylvania's farmers still bless his name. Not only were roads improved but unemployment during the Great Depression was eased by the use of a minimum of machinery and a maximum of hand labor, with priority given to

needy persons recommended by local relief boards.

As in the heydays of the canal and the railroad, Harrisburg was an intersecting point and center for state and national highways. During the 1920s and 1930s an almost weekly chore of Pennsylvania's governors was their official appearances at the opening of some newly constructed section of road. Lincoln Highway, Routes 5, 11, 15, 22, 30, and 322 became familiar terms to motorists. And in 1940 the Pennsylvania Turnpike opened its toll booths and Harrisburgers had only to drive to the outskirts of the city to get onto the 160-mile, 4-lane superhighway.

World War II temporarily "froze" this highway system. Curtailment of road construction, gasoline rationing, lowering of speed limits, and discontinuance of civilian car and truck manufacture kept would-be travelers marking time during the war years. But that interval was only a prelude to later giant steps forward in highway construction —but in an era outside the scope of this book.

Harrisburg's memorial to the soldiers and sailors who gave their lives to preserve the Union took the form of an Egyptian obelisk of Susquehanna granite. It was designed by a local architect, E. Worall Hudson, who was paid $100 for his services. Constructed in 1866-67, it enhanced the intersection of Second and State streets for ninety years. Increasing automobile traffic and numerous accidents caused its removal to the present site at Fourth and Division streets.

Chapter 8

Harrisburg's First Forty Years as a City

On March 19, 1860, Harrisburg was incorporated as a city; thirteen months later on April 12, 1861, Confederate guns opened fire on Fort Sumter in the Charleston, South Carolina harbor and plunged the nation into the four-year agony of the Civil War. Less than two months before, on Washington's birthday, February 22, Harrisburg had enthusiastically welcomed President-elect Abraham Lincoln on his journey from Springfield, Illinois to Washington. He had stayed briefly at the Jones House on the Square; word of a planned assassination attempt in Baltimore had sent him on secretly to the nation's capital for his inauguration.

Harrisburg responded nobly to the President's several calls for men during the four years of the war. A painstaking search through the pages of the five fat volumes of Bates' *History of Pennsylvania Volunteers* yields the following information: companies recruited solely in Harrisburg, 12; from Dauphin County, 19; from the city, Dauphin County, and other towns and counties, 13. Figuring an enlisted company's strength at 100, it may be seen that the city furnished at the very least about 1200 men—substantial contribution, considering its 1860 population of 13,405.

From the start Harrisburg was a war center. In the city's Camp Curtin (named for war Governor Andrew Gregg Curtin) recruited men assembled, not only from Pennsylvania but from many other Northern states as well, to be sworn into service, receive equipment, be drilled, and finally sent off to Union armies in the East and West. The city also served as a supply depot, receiving and distributing thousands of tons of war materiel. A large corral of government horses was maintained where the old Graupner brewery later stood, on Market Street above the subway.

The city lived through two especially thrilling periods in the war. The first came in September, 1862, when Lee crossed the Potomac on his first invasion. Harrisburgers did not need to be reminded that their city was a prime target for the Confederates. Hundreds of volunteers swarmed into Camp Curtin; hundreds of others crossed the river to work on fortifications on the West Shore. Fortunately, the crisis was short-lived; the Battle of Antietam on September 17 crippled Lee and sent his army back into Virginia.

But the brief Maryland invasion and its attendant alarm was only a foretaste of the real thing. Fresh from his brilliant victory at Chancellorsville in early May, 1863, Lee again moved north with a larger army. By the middle of June, Union Army engineers were hurriedly laying out defense lines on the West Shore, and building Forts Washington and Couch on the ridge beyond the western end of the Market Street camelback bridge. Shirt-sleeved citizens labored with blistered hands to throw up entrenchments. Troops arrived from New York by train and were marched across the bridge to help man the defense lines. The climax came on June 29 with a brief skirmish at Oyster's Point in Camp Hill. Here the Trindle Spring Road and the Carlisle Pike converged to make one road to the camelback bridge. The Union forces held, the Confederates drew back and, receiving belated orders on the thirtieth, marched away toward Gettysburg. This was the real high-water mark of the Confederacy; no other organized Confederate unit got so far north.

Thereafter the tide receded, with Gettysburg marking the war's turning point. Harrisburg boys in blue fought out the

The accompanying artist's sketch published in a nationally circulated magazine during Civil War days pictures Union Army volunteers drilling at Camp Curtin, located north of Maclay Street, between the railroad and the river. Just how authentic it is as to details is questionable.

Medical personnel and Union Army soldiers are pictured in this pen-and-ink sketch of the U.S. Army Hospital at Camp Curtin. The building was still standing abandoned in the early 1880s, according to Gus M. Steinmetz, who played about it as a boy.

remaining two bloody years until Lee's surrender brought an end. Then came the tragedy of Lincoln's assassination, and on April 21, 1865, the body of the martyred President came to Harrisburg to lie in state for the night in the House of Representatives chamber in the Capitol. All through a night of drenching rain a double line of mourning citizens passed for a last reverent look at the man who had saved the Union.

The war really ended for Harrisburg with the homecoming of its veterans. Citizens erected a huge, three-story-high, flag-decorated arch on the Square, inscribed with the names of thirty-six states; Pennsylvania's name marked the keystone. Signs like "Welcome! the Brave!" hung on stores and homes as the citizen-soldiers marched through the arch on their way to mustering out at Camp Curtin.

In 1869 Harrisburg and Dauphin County honored their soldiers and sail-ors with a tall obelisk (one-fifth the height of the Washington Monument) at State and Second streets. In the late 1950s it fell victim to progress. It had become increasingly a traffic hazard, so city officials had it taken down and re-erected, stone for stone, on the William Penn High School campus.

To present a *full* history of Harrisburg for the period 1860-1950 is outside the scope of this book. Merely listing the names of prominent citizens who figured in Harrisburg's growth, the tabulating of societies and organizations—civic, cultural, historical, fraternal, religious, and the like—its hospitals, its banks, its industries, and its myriad changes and improvements would tax the capacity of even a small encyclopedia. Therefore this and the following chapter are necessarily confined to items arbitrarily selected and which are deemed of the broadest interest—with apologies for such omissions as may

Children born to the pioneering Rutherford family carried their devotion to the land they settled far into their lives. They were successful in their chosen professions and active in civic affairs over a long period of time. Some, like Capt. John Park Rutherford, donned uniforms and fought for their country.

Besides serving in the military, Rutherford, born 1803, was a farmer, superintendent of the Wiconisco Canal, auditor, jury commissioner, and vice-president of the Pennsylvania Agricultural Society. He died in 1871.

raise outraged or anguished outcries from those with more specialized interests.

At the start of the 1860s Harrisburg was still a small town. Its bounds and population (13,405) seemed scarcely to entitle it to cityhood. Housing ended at about North Street; beyond were only meadows and a few farms. Eastward, Allison's Hill could count only a half-dozen houses. In spite of being the state capital, the city was still something of a "one-horse town."

But because Harrisburg *was* the capital, it entertained many distinguished visitors, and has done so ever since. On October 2 and 3, 1860, Albert Edward, Prince of Wales and later King Edward VII, stopped at the Jones House. President Andrew Johnson, Lieutenant General U. S. Grant, and Admiral David G.

Farragut were in the city September 14 and 15, 1866; they stayed at the old Bolton Hotel on the Square. Later Grant returned as ex-President from his world tour on December 15, 1879, and was entertained by Governor Henry M. Hoyt. The dedication of the new Capitol on October 4, 1906, brought President Theodore Roosevelt to deliver the dedicatory address. And to round out an admittedly incomplete list it should be mentioned that there were presidential campaign visits to the city by Franklin D. Roosevelt in 1936 and John F. Kennedy in 1960; as President, Kennedy returned in 1962.

Harrisburg had its first street railway in 1861 when the Harrisburg Passenger Railway Company ran a horse-car line on Third Street from Walnut to Broad. Other lines later served to the east and south. Horse-car transport continued until as late as 1892. But in 1888 the march of progress brought electrification of the trolley lines. Harrisburg missed by less than half a year being the first city to electrify its street railways; Richmond, Virginia was the first.

The first electric line ran from Harrisburg to Steelton; the city system began operation in 1891. Many old-timers remember the fun of placing pennies on the track to be flattened with resounding thumps by the trolley wheels, accompanied by annoyed objurgations from motorman and conductor. In summer open cars were used. The same old-timers will recall the sight of those cars during the crowded homeward rush hour, the seats full and passengers clustered on the long running boards. Or the excitement of "hooking a ride" by pedaling a bicycle up behind a trolley and clutching the raised "cowcatcher" while avoiding the stern eye of the conductor.

Time eventually caught up with the street car; the rails today are paved over (where they were not taken up) and the malodorous bus has replaced the clanging trolley.

In 1865 the city suffered another of its seemingly almost perennial floods (42 were recorded in 190 years), in which South Harrisburg was—as usual!— inundated with accompanying loss of outhouses and fences. Undaunted, the Shipokers drained their cellars, replaced their losses, and defiantly awaited the next high water.

By 1870 city population had almost doubled the 1860 figure—it was up to 23,000. The city had expanded correspondingly; it had been built up to Twelfth Street from the river and extended as far north as Maclay. This

and Joseph Jefferson among them. The Opera House flourished as a center of Harrisburg's cultural life until fire destroyed it in 1907.

The State Street Bridge was erected and a city fire alarm system was also installed in 1873. The new bridge over the P.R.R. tracks provided another direct route to Allison's Hill, and confirmed the city's steady eastward expansion. The fire alarm system enabled the many volunteer fire companies to respond more quickly to the numerous fires that plagued the city during this period.

A listing of the fires during Harrisburg's first fifty years reads almost like a

Harrisburg's second Pennsylvania Railroad passenger station was in the process of being razed in 1887 when the accompanying photograph was taken showing the main entrance to the waiting room and ticket offices, facing Market Street. The big train shed that had joined the two sections of the building had been removed and work had been started on the present station.

added some 500 acres to the city area, which, combined with about 50 acres of streets and houses on Allison's Hill and a considerable acreage south from Paxton Street, now spread nearly double its early size.

The year 1873 saw the opening of the Grand Opera House on the southeast corner of Third and Walnut streets, the site of the later Penn-Harris Hotel. Many famous actors and singers appeared on its stage, Madam Mojeska

roll call of its industries: Trullinger's planing mill, Fleming's coach shop, King's hardware store, Dunlap's Golden Lamb Hotel, Toner's livery stable, Franklin Iron Works, Harrisburg Car Manufacturing Company (twice), Lochiel Iron Works, State Printing Office, Harrisburg Foundry and Machine Works (twice), Eby's Coal Elevator, Hartman's tannery, a knitting factory, Monaghan-Bay Shoe Factory, Laverty's furniture store, Ensminger lumber yard, Pipe and Pipe Bending Works (twice), and the Boll Manufacturing Company.

The number of large fires plus the population growth made a new reservoir necessary. For increased water pressure a 210-foot standpipe was erected near the riverside pumping station in 1876. With its cone-shaped top it made a notable feature of the city's skyline.

On the Fourth of July, 1876, Harrisburg celebrated the nation's centennial. The Odd Fellows and the Fire Department took charge of the biggest parade the city had witnessed up to that time. Following this spectacle a meeting was held in the Capitol's House of Representatives. A. Boyd Hamilton presided, just-retired first Superintendent of Schools Samuel D. Ingram read the Dec-

laration of Independence, and Hamilton, Dr. Thomas Robinson, and Dr. William H. Egle delivered patriotic addresses.

The railroad riots of July, 1877, furnished Harrisburg with the most excitement it had experienced since the Confederate invasion threat of '63. Elite "City Grays" (the new name for the old "First City Zouaves" of 1861) went on duty at once to guard the State Arsenal.

So great was the fear that the rioters would seize the Arsenal and arm themselves that the Seventh and Eighth Regiments were sent to reinforce the "Grays." Armed citizens patrolled the streets, but the scare evaporated when a trainload supposedly consisting of railroaders threatening to burn the city

Horse cars, long skirts, and high-buttoned shoes were quite the thing in 1880 when a cameraman recorded this scene at the northeast corner of Market Square. An afternoon sun cast lengthening shadows of the diminutive street cars and a nearby fire plug on the uneven brick surface of the pavement. Across the Square the dry goods and carpet store of Sol Kuhn invited customers to stop in.

Growing with the city, the daily and weekly Telegraph *(the weekly edition was mainly for rural subscribers), first under the guidance of George Bergner, a bookseller living and doing business at 51 Market Street, and later his son, Charles H., moved into the newspaper's own building at Third and Market streets in 1874. The building is still there, but the* Telegraph *newspaper is long gone, leaving its "print" in the sands of time–a third Telegraph Building facing Federal Square, on Locust Street, and the Telegraph Press, a commercial printing plant now on North Cameron Street.*

turned out to be a less ambitious element which was easily dispersed.

The 1880s was an eventful decade in the city's life. Harrisburg scored another "first" when the Wednesday Club was founded in 1881 and officially organized in May 1882. It is the oldest musical organization in the nation in point of continuous existence. It now has a program of student and member recitals and it presents a yearly schedule of concerts by professional artists. These are held in the Forum of the State Education Building—but usually *not* on Wednesday!

In the summer of 1885 Harrisburg celebrated its own centennial with display of flags, parades, orations, and fireworks. Street paving began in earnest, and the Light, Heat & Power Company provided electric light from

their generating plant on Fourth Street near South.

The spring of 1886 brought another flood with attendant damage in South Harrisburg. In the fall, the Harrisburg Steam Heat & Power Company incorporated, but steam was not turned on until November, 1887. In the summer of 1887, a new Cumberland Valley Railroad bridge was finally completed— almost fifty years after the first bridge went into service in 1839. During that time the bridge burned, was rebuilt, and was several times renovated and strengthened. It is Harrisburg's oldest railroad bridge.

Another bridge went up in 1888, the Mulberry Street viaduct, to carry the increased traffic to and from the rapidly growing Allison's Hill section. The first bridge was of steel girder construction,

Mail delivery in Harrisburg was ably handled by twelve carriers in 1885. Here they are, posed on the steps of the then new Post Office at Third and Walnut streets, ready to start their rounds:

Robert Ensminger (in white) was superintendent of mails. Carriers, front row, l. to r., Ira P. Knouse, Richard H. Weaver, John Neidig, and E. C. Kutz. Rear row, l. to r., Charles E. Troweck, Cameron McCormick, Nelson Lukens, D. H. Hamaker, David Shelly, George Jackson, Robert Ensminger, and Andrew Jackson.

with iron railings and wooden floor and sidewalk. As on-the-spot fire protection, barrels of water were placed at intervals along the sidewalk, but they were of little use when flames and sparks from the Boll Manufacturing Company fire in 1907 engulfed the wooden roadway and reduced the girders and rails to twisted scrap iron. Construction of the present reinforced concrete bridge began almost at once.

On June 2, 1889, the Susquehanna flooded again, the water cresting at 27 feet 1 inch above low water mark. South Harrisburgers took refuge in their second floors and boats went from window to window rescuing marooned families. Also this year, the market sheds which were for so long a feature of the Square were removed to make way for street railway tracks.

If Harrisburg has a sentimental favorite among its bridges it must surely be the Walnut Street bridge—opened for use on April 25, 1890. Affectionately called "Old Shaky"—and no one who has walked across it during the passage

of car and truck traffic will ask why—it withstood floods and the battering of ice which carried away parts of its neighbor and rival, the camelback Market Street bridge. Even the tremendous flood of 1936 could do little more than bend its guardrails. It is a Harrisburg landmark and justly entitled to its status as a National Historic Place.

In 1891 the telephone came to Harrisburg with the incorporation of the Southern Pennsylvania Telephone Company. The first phones were wall instruments. One took the receiver off a Y-shaped hook, swung the transmitter ("the thing you talk into") down to mouth level, turning a little crank vigorously, and waited breathlessly for the operator's "Number, please." In those first years the children of households blessed with phones were kept busy running to neighbors with messages or summons to answer calls. Those with a phone suffered from popularity.

The same year saw the completion of another bridge, the Philadelphia & Reading's. This brought the city's

Members of the Harrisburg Boat Club, apparently apprehensive of the dangers posed by an ice flood of 1888, gather to move their craft from buildings threatened by moving ice on the river opposite Independence Island.

cross-river bridge total to four.

The Harrisburg Choral Society was formed in 1895 as an outlet and display case for the city's vocal talent. Members rehearse weekly for the Christmas and spring concerts that have become a feature of Harrisburg's musical life. After thirteen years under the direction of Philadelphian W. W. Gilchrist, the society performed under the leadership of Professor Edwin J. DeCevee, a great name in Harrisburg music. Since 1956 Donald L. Clapper has been the popular and very talented director.

The last three years of the nineteenth century went out—both figuratively and literally—with a flash and a bang. The flash came with the fire that burned the old Capitol on February 2, 1897. It was one of Harrisburg's most spectacular blazes. The legislators moved into the Grace Methodist Church, as mentioned earlier, and among other things voted down a bill to remove the capital to Philadelphia. Rebuilding plans were started almost immediately. (See next chapter.)

It is an odd fact that the woman whose name came to be associated with outstanding service to Harrisburg during this period and for many years afterward was not a native of the city and did not come here until 1889. Mrs. Lyman D. Gilbert, whose husband was also a notable civic leader, was born and lived in Petersburg, Virginia until her marriage. Perhaps her most notable and enduring contribution to Harrisburg was her organization and long leadership of the Civic Club. January 21, 1898, is a date to remember with gratitude; the city is the richer for what grew from that first meeting in the Gilbert home at 203 Front Street. To list all of Mrs. Gilbert's con-

Fading from the local scene on a day in 1889, the market sheds which early gave their name to the city's business center were being razed when the accompanying picture was taken. A group of boys play around the ruins while two men, probably recalling memories of another day, look over the scene.

Harrisburg's second National Guard Armory, at Second and Forster streets, was opened for use February 18, 1885. It occupied the former site of the J. S. Meserau Lumber Yard (1875), and the land on which it stood was donated by Mrs. Sara Haldeman Haley. The armory was destroyed by fire in May, 1932.

tributions to the community would be to name every philanthropic project undertaken in the first thirty years or more of the present century. No committee was considered complete without her. The Kiwanis Club's medal, awarded to the person performing the greatest service to Harrisburg, was first presented to Mrs. Gilbert.

(An interesting sidelight concerns Lyman Gilbert. He was a big man, both in community affairs and in physique. The specially built bathtub in his home was reputedly the largest in Harrisburg.)

The century neared its close with a bang. On February 15, 1898 the U.S.S. *Maine* was blown up in Havana Harbor; on April 21, 1898, the United States went to war with Spain, chanting the slogan "Remember the *Maine!*" Volunteers poured into Harrisburg; the City Grays and the Governor's Troop joined other Pennsylvania soldiers at Camp Hastings, Mount Gretna (named for Governor Daniel H. Hastings), and more troops assembled at Camp Meade,

Middletown. Soldiers on leave from the latter camp swarmed Harrisburg streets and local women ran a "Soldiers' Rest" on Walnut Street, a forerunner of later wars' USO's. The Spanish-American War was America's shortest war; the Treaty of Paris on December 10, 1898, ended hostilities and Harrisburg's soldiers returned to resume peacetime activities.

The organization of two women's groups marked the last year of the century: the Daughters of 1812, and the Visiting Nurses' Association.

In its first forty years as a city, Harrisburg had known the excitement of two wars, had contested as best it could with the perils of fire and flood, and was on the brink of a new era which would capitalize on the advantages of electricity and the telephone. The city continued to grow, both culturally and in physical size. With the beginning of the twentieth century Harrisburg was to move toward its goal of "City Beautiful." Civic improvement was in the air.

A center for cultural activities in the city
was the old Grand Opera House that had
been opened to the public in 1876. Scene of
theatrical presentations, social events,
graduation exercises, and even political
meetings, it served its purpose well until
the night of February 1, 1907, when it was
completely destroyed in a spectacular
blaze reminiscent of one that had destroyed the State Capitol a decade previously.

Steam engines of all sizes and shapes were
once manufactured in Harrisburg. One of
the firms engaged in this business was the
Harrisburg Car Manufacturing Company,
which later became the Harrisburg Foundry & Machine Company. An 1880 portable model is shown here in a company advertisement.

PAXTON
Portable Steam Engin

BUILT BY
HARRISBURG CAR MANUFACTURING
THE
MOST DESIRABLE PORTABLE ENGIN
IN THE MARKET
FOR

The man who provided many of the photographs for this book, William Stoey, stands in the center (rear, wearing a white bow tie) of a family group who posed for the portrait one day long ago in the backyard of his home at 1201 North Front Street.

Horsepower of a kind different from that used today provided the means for accomplishing much of the work around the farm of yesterday. Walking behind the plow while his young daughter watches is one of the many farmers who provided the city with homegrown produce on sale at the various farmers' markets of yesterday.

"The smith, a mighty man is he" (Longfellow). The poet was referring to the local blacksmith of yesteryear depicted in the above photo.

Reuben Bowers, 336 Hummel Street, operated one of the several smithies in the city in 1898 and his was typical of such neighborhood industries of that day.

In 1885 Harrisburg boasted 250 telephones serviced by the Harrisburg Telephone Exchange Company, a subsidiary of the Pennsylvania Telephone Company, with exchanges in Steelton, Middletown, and Lancaster. Monthly "rent" for a telephone was three dollars, and Horace A. Clute was the general manager. The office was located at 20 North Fourth Street.

Harrisburg, Pa., _____, 18

To Harrisburg Telephonic Exchange Co., D

H. A. CLUTE, General Manager.

For rent of _____ Telephone from _____ to _____, $_____

EXCHANGES IN
Harrisburg,   Lancaster,
Steelton,   Middletown.

Received Payment,

General Mana

The flood of '89 was receding although logs were still jammed in the lower girders of the Cumberland Valley Railroad bridge here. Following inspection by railroad officials, the first train in two days (pictured in the photograph) was allowed to cross to the West Shore and continue its way down the valley to Hagerstown.

Bicycle races were popular among Harrisburg's sports fans prior to the advent of the automobile. A favorite spot for these events until the early 1900s was the Harrisburg Driving Park, located along River Road north of what is now Division Street.

The above photo, taken about the turn of the century, shows one such event about to get underway with contestants and their assistants at the starting line.

Spectators braved a February blizzard to watch the old Capitol Building pass into history as the result of a consuming fire in 1897. Although it was never proven to have been of incendiary origin, suspicions of political infighting pointed in that direction.

The tail end of a circus parade passes through Market Square on a summer day in 1892. Note the steam calliope between the last two wagons and the crowd breaking up as delivery wagons resume their rounds.

The end of an era is represented as the last horse car in Harrisburg, operated by the Harrisburg Passenger Railway, prepares to leave its terminal at Sixth and Maclay streets on a summer day in 1892. The driver, Curtis Chronister, gave up his driving reins for the controls of an electric car and worked for successor companies for many years thereafter. In the background is the long-gone Maple Grove Hotel, a favorite gathering place for horse traders of the day.

Most Harrisburg homes where children lived during the waning years of the last century celebrated the Christmas holidays with a gaily decorated tree set in a diorama like that shown below. Augustus Wildman, a well-known local contractor, called in Stoey, the photographer, to record the 1896 event.

Boyish sport along the river's edge provided as much of a thrill long ago as it does today. Fishing or skipping stones on the surface of the water was a fun thing for the group of boys gathered at Dintaman's Boat Livery. Steamboats in the background were a part of the coal fleet and the huge smoke stack and water tower in the distance were located at the City Pumping Station, Front and North streets.

What the well-dressed man wore in the 1890s was available at J. E. Hemperly's haberdashery. Note the unique suspender display incorporating an umbrella bearing the proprietor's name, the stiff collar white shirts, the straw "skimmers" (hats) on a shelf to the left, and other items of male dress. Store accessories included the large gaslight fixture, the glass showcases, and the balls of string for tying packages in cast-iron cages hanging from the ceiling.

The day of the huckster in Harrisburg is long past. He and his horse-drawn wagon loaded with fruit and vegetables would not get a block from home in this day of fast motor traffic. Long ago on a sunny day in the 1890s such was not the case as this unknown mobile merchant peddled his stock of watermelons along an uptown street.

Hogentogler's store at Third and Boas streets was long a haven for husbands seeking surcease from the vicissitudes of home life on a day off from the job. At the rear of the storeroom, close to the stove, kegs, stools, and boxes provided facilities for ongoing games of cards and checkers, complete with kibitzers. Apparently the spectators hesitated to identify themselves for personal reasons, as the photographer did not list them.

Toll gates are still around today just as they were back in 1895 when Mr. Stoey set up his camera to record this scene of action at a toll gate along the river road, north of the city.

Note the female tolltaker patiently waiting while one of the men in the carriage digs into his pocket for a coin. The man with the bicycle seems in no hurry. Maybe he doesn't have any toll in his pocket, but more than likely he is just taking time out to socialize with the toll collector.

Spanish-American war veterans enjoyed refreshment and relaxation at the "Soldiers Rest," Court and Walnut streets. The 1898 "USO" occupied a brick building built in 1815 by the County Commissioners and used as a court house until 1822. Today the site is occupied by the Kline Building.

The troopers gathered for their picture are probably on leave from Camp Meade, near Middletown.

President William McKinley and Mrs. McKinley paid a visit to Camp Meade to review U.S. troops returning from the Spanish-American War, September, 1898. Here the President and his wife, accompanied by their bodyguards, walk towards the reviewing stand as a crowd of curious spectators look on and a man on the extreme right tips his hat as a gesture of honor. Mrs. McKinley's personal maid follows as a bright sun casts shadows (of portent?) on the rough pathway.

Model boats, not model airplanes, automobiles, or space ships occupied the attention of youth and adult alike eighty years ago. Here is a model of the famous battleship Maine *with a miniature sailboat nearby as they were floating on the surface of the Susquehanna at the foot of Herr Street long ago.*

Birthday celebrations take many forms, but when an adult comes up with a fiftieth anniversary of his arrival on this planet, certain similarities exist between those in the 1890s and today. This refers to the refreshments served, not the attire of the guests or the surroundings. Such was the case when B. I. Lingle, a local painting contractor, celebrated his attainment of that milestone together with his family and guests.

Dr. C. A. Rather, onetime prominent local physician, made his rounds in a rubber-tired buggy, drawn by a team of high-stepping horses and driven by an immaculately attired, dark-skinned groom. The good doctor paused long enough at Third and Maclay streets for his picture to be taken. In the background is the Eby mansion.

Sunday outings for many Harrisburg families in the 1890s consisted of bicycle jaunts to nearby points. A favorite trip was up along the river to Dauphin. Here the camera records such an outing by the Cook family as they arrived at the old stone bridge spanning Clark's Creek, north of the town which bears the name of the county in which it is situated.

For many years the steam ferryboat Kingfisher plied the surface of the Susquehanna between Harrisburg and West Fairview, except when ice clogged the waterway. Traffic was quite good, commutation tickets for regular patrons were issued. Service continued until the "Hardscrabble" area was torn down to make way for the sunken gardens along Front Street in the 1920s. The accompanying photo shows the Kingfisher and its substitute at dock on the West Shore.

Popguns complete with corks, toy horses on wheels, high-button shoes, and "Little Lord Fauntleroy" suits were quite the thing back in 1898. Young Cyrus Weaver looks with some apprehension at the big black box pointed in his direction by a man hiding his head under a black cloth.

Mud in ample quantities was a part of over-the-road travel in the Harrisburg area around the turn of the century, as the above photo, taken in the Lemoyne "bottleneck," indicates. In those days, before the advent of the auto and even the street car, the location was known as "the cut." Traffic consisted of horse-drawn vehicles, bicycles, and pedestrians in numbers which did not create a "bottleneck."

Katherine and Clara Stoey model winter styles of the times in the backyard of their home at 1201 North Front Street, on a cold day in 1895. Are the hats homemade creations, or that of a prominent milliner of that period?

HARRISBURG TO WINCHESTER

	*No. 1	*No. 3	†No. 5	*No. 7	†No. 9	*No. 11	*No. 13
Lv. New York (Penn'a Sta.)	d9.00 pm	12.45 am	....	10.04 am	....	.... pm	5.30 pm
" Philadelphia...	11.45	4.20	8.10	11.50	....	i 4.58	8.11
" Baltimore U D.	11.25	4.05	8.55	1.00	....	4.20	8.35
Lv. Harrisburg....	5.05 am	7.52 am	11.59 am	‡2.38 pm	5.45 pm	7.55 pm	11.10 pm
Ar. Lemoyne....f	r a..	r a..	r	v a....	5.50	a	....
" White Hill....f	r a..	r a..	....	....	5.53	a	....
" Shiremans'n f	r b	g b..	....	v b..	5.57	b....	....
" Mechanicsburg	5.26	8.12	12.16	3.57	6.04	8.11	11.26
" Dillsburg....	†6.25	†9.30	12.45	4.25	6.28	....	....
" New Kingst'n f	*5.33	*8.19	12.23	4.04	6.10	b....	b....
" Gettysb'g Jc..f	....	....	....	....	h..	....	....
" Carlisle......	5.49	8.34	12.36	4.17	6.26	8.29	11.42
" Greason....f	5.58	8.43	12.44	4.25	6.26	8.37	b....
" Alterton....f	b....	8.46	....	b....	6.40	b....	....
" Newville......	6.10	8.54	12.55	4.35	6.48	8.46	12.00
" Oakville....f	6.18	9.01	1.02	4.43	6.55	8.53	....
" Shippensburg.	6.31	9.14	1.14	4.55	7.07	9.05	12.18
" Scotland....f	6.42	9.24	1.24	5.06	7.17	9.16	....
" Chambersburg.	6.49	9.31	1.30	5.12	7.23	9.22	12.34
" Waynesboro..	§8.29	10.38	2.20	6.01	....	10.05	....
" Marion......f	*t....	10.29	....	1.41	t....	7.34	9.34
" Mercersburg..	†8.31	10.29	....	6.07	....	....	....
" Greencastle...	*7.16	9.52	1.49	5.34	7.41	9.41	12.50
" Mason-Dixon f	7.25	10.02	1.57	5.42	7.49	9.49	...
" Maugansville f	7.30	10.07	2.02	5.46	7.53	b....	....
Ar. Hagerstown..	7.40	10.14	2.10	5.55	8.01	10.00	1.07
Lv. Hagerstown...	†7.48	10.19	....	6.00	....	....	....
Ar. Williamsport f	7.59	10.30	....	6.11	....	....	....
" Fall'g Waters f	8.08	10.38	....	6.20	....	....	....
" Bedington ...f	8.16	10.44	....	6.26	....	....	....
" Martinsburg ..	8.34	10.59	....	6.42	....	....	....
" Inwood ......f	8.50	11.15	....	6.58	....	....	....
" Bunker Hill .f	8.54	11.19	....	7.02	....	....	....
" Clearbrook...f	9.06	11.31	....	7.14	....	....	....
Ar. Winchester...	9.20 am	11.45 am	pm	7.27 pm	pm	pm	am

WINCHESTER TO HARRISBURG

	*No. 2	†No. 4	*No. 6	*No. 8	*No. 10	†No. 12	*No. 14
Lv. Winchester...	am	am	7.25 am	pm	2.20 pm	5.37 pm	pm
" Clearbrook...f	....	....	7.36	....	2.32	5.48	....
" Bunker Hill .f	....	....	7.49	....	2.43	6.00	....
" Inwood ......f	....	....	7.54	....	2.47	6.05	....
" Martinsburg ..	....	....	8.11	....	3.05	6.22	....
" Bedington ...f	....	....	8.26	....	3.18	6.35	....
" Valley Waters f	....	....	8.32	....	3.24	6.41	....
" Williamsport f	....	....	8.43	....	3.33	6.51	....
Ar. Hagerstown...	....	....	8.57	....	3.46	7.04	....
Lv. Hagerstown...	2.25	7.05	9.03	12.25	3.52	7.09	10.20
" Maugansville f	....	7.13	9.12	12.32	4.01	7.17	b....
" Mason-Dixon f	....	7.17	9.16	12.36	4.05	7.21	10.41
" Greencastle...	2.43	7.25	9.26	12.46	4.16	7.29	10.49
" Mercersburg ..	....	....	8.09	†12.05	3.83	....	....
" Marion......f	....	7.34	h b..	h b..	h..	....	10 58
" Waynesboro..	....	6.55	§8.44	†12.10	3.40	6.25	10.25
" Chambersburg.	3.00	7.44	*9.50	*1.06	4.42	7.49	11.10
" Scotland....f	....	7.52	9.59	1.13	4.50	7.56	11.18
" Shippensburg.	3.17	8.03	10.10	1.26	5.02	8.07	11.80
" Oakville....f	....	8.13	10.20	1.87	5.12	8.17	11.38
" Newville......	3.34	8.24	10.25	1.46	5.20	8.24	11.47
" Alterton....f	....	8.31	b..	b...	5.27	....	b ...
" Greason....f	....	8.35	10.38	1.55	5.31	8.33	b..
" Carlisle......	3.51	8.44	10.48	2.04	5.40	8.42	12.06
" Gettysb'g Jc..f	....	....	....	....	....	....	....
" New Kingst'n f	....	....	b..	b...	5.50	8.51	b....
" Dillsburg......	....	8.25	10.30	1.40	5.15	....	....
" Mechanicsburg	4.07	9.00	11.05	2.20	5.59	8.58	12.24
" Shiremanst'n f	....	....	u b..	b....	u b..	u....	b....
" White Hill...f	....	....	....	....	....	....	c....
" Lemoyne....f	....	....	u c..	c....	u c..	....	c....
Ar. Harrisburg...	4.22 am	9.15 am	11.20 am	2.35 pm	6.17 pm	9.15 am	12.40 am
Ar. Baltimore U D.	8.10	12.05	3.25	6.05	11.05	2.20	8.10
" Philadelphia ..	e 7.19	12.01	†2.80	5.25	9.20	11.50	4.12
" New York (Penn'a Sta.)	9.28 am	2.00 pm	†5.00 pm	8.00 pm	11.50 pm	am	7.50 am

* Daily. † Daily except Sunday. § Sunday only.

‡ Train No. 7 also has connection from Penn'a Limited, train No. 5 leaving New York 11.04 A.M., Philadelphia 1.11 P.M.

Pullman All Steel Sleeping Cars on trains 1 and 13 west and 2 and 14 east daily. Parlor Cars on No. 4 east and No. 11 west daily except Sunday.

a At stations marked "a" trains scheduled to leave starting point before midnight of Sunday will stop to receive passengers on signal or on notice to agent.

b At stations marked "b" trains scheduled to leave starting point before midnight of Sunday will stop to receive or discharge passengers on signal or on notice to agent or conductor.

c At stations marked "c" trains scheduled to leave starting point before midnight of Sunday will stop to discharge passengers on notice to conductor.

d New York and Hagerstown Sleeper leaves New York 8.00 P.M.

e Time at North Philadelphia.

f At stations marked "f" trains will stop when time is given only on signal or notice to Agent or Conductor unless otherwise noted.

g Stop to receive passengers on signal or on notice to agent.

h Stop to discharge passengers on notice to conductors.

i On Sunday leaves New York 2.08 P.M., Philadelphia 4.32 P.M.

r Stop on signal to receive passengers for Carlisle and stations west of Carlisle.

t Stop to receive passengers for Greencastle or stations west of Greencastle.

u Stop to discharge passengers from stations west of Carlisle.

v Stops on signal to receive passengers for stations west of Carlisle.

In the heyday of the railroads the Cumberland Valley Railroad offered fairly frequent service between this city, Hagerstown, Maryland and Winchester, Virginia, as indicated in the reproduction of an 1887 public timetable.

Bicycles were a popular mode of transportation back in the 1890s just as they are today. George McFarland, who later became one of Harrisburg's first automobile dealers, sold a lot of them. Below is a McFarland display at a local exposition.

George was a brother of J. Horace McFarland, famed rose fancier, and prominent proprietor of a large printing concern here, the Mt. Pleasant Press.

Dr. J. H. Fager not only was an excellent physician and prominent citizen, he also was a horticulturist of note. This excellent portrait is of the good doctor busy with his favorite hobby in the garden of his home. The year: 1897.

J. R. Stoey's customers relax in comfort as they select wallpaper patterns of the day at his place of business on North Third Street in 1895. Note their attire. The man wears a heavy topcoat and derby hat, while his wife is protected by a long, dark cape with matching flat-brimmed hat. It must have been a cold day.

Prominent on the back wall is Stoey's identification, partially obscured by a supporting pillar and a fancy gas lamp fixture.

The former grade crossing just east of Fifth and Market streets was such a dangerous place that a crowd of curious citizens gathered to watch a brave photographer set up his camera on the railroad tracks to take a picture of the trackside European Hotel, locally named "The Steamboat" because of its nautical appearance. The date: 1899.

One of the local industries that flourished in the early years of this century was the Harrisburg Foundry & Machine Works, an outgrowth of the former Harrisburg Car Manufacturing Company. Here are a group of F&M workers.

Harry Bowman (second row, left end) was foreman. Others are unidentified except Emanuel Myers (fifth from the left, rear row), who later was promoted to a foreman's position, and the man in the third row with an "X" on his shirt, who was a brother of Governor Hastings.

It is 1890. The ancient market sheds that gave the Square its name and the little horse cars have passed into history. Electric trolley cars are now carrying the public to all parts of the city and even into the suburbs. But further changes are to come with the passing years. Only the ancient Bolton House (now the Warner Hotel) would survive to the present. The hotel has been designated a National Historic Landmark.

Another photo from the Stoey collection is this interesting but not identified one, taken apparently in the backyard of one of his neighbor's homes. A notation on the original states only "two sisters fight over 'Chestnuts' " —which could have been the nickname of their baby brother.

In 1886 natural ice was the main summer staple for cooling and preserving food and drink. It was a big business then, big enough for ice dealers to have their own private railroad cars and large storage facilities.

H. A. W. Walkemeyer, of Harrisburg, was one, and his ice dam and ice house with its railroad siding was located at Ellendale Forge, along Stony Creek near Dauphin.

If you had climbed the steeple of the Market Square Presbyterian Church on a day in 1885, this is what you would have seen from your high perch. Looking east towards Allison's Hill, you would have noted long-vanished buildings bordering Blackberry Alley, Chestnut Street, Fourth Street, and the railroad. The church steeple on the left is that of Zion Lutheran Church; that on the lower right, Salem Reformed (now Salem United Church of Christ). Both have survived the passing years. The huge train shed, center left, was under construction at the time. It also is still in use, but its life span is limited by the city's redevelopment plans.

On a very special day in 1896, sixth-grade pupils at Harris Park School together with their teacher, Miss Sees, assembled on the front steps of that long-vanished building to have their picture taken.

Front row, l. to r.: Florence Smith, Anne Saunders, Bertha Bently, Jennie Miller, Theresa Maguire, Mary Sheesley, Mollie Kirkland, Jennie Swartz, and Esther Maxwell.

Second row: Bertha Berry, Mary Sprout, Clara Walkemeyer, Mabel Walkemeyer, Mabel Swanberry, Clara Roberts, Ella Stair, and Bertha Shull.

Third row: Emma Forsyth, Florence Miller, Carrie Manum, Elsie Zimmerman, and Jennie Martin.

Fourth row: Walter Lewis, Earl Anderson, Clara Leeds, Mary Maley, Esther Sellers, Emma Swartz, Frank Parks, William Walkemeyer, and Ralph Essig.

Fifth row: William Hoffman, Robert Tippett, Robert Breece, Clarence Gibbons, Charles Kautz, Charles Biery, and Charles Maley.

Only a shell of Pennsylvania's first permanent headquarters remained standing following a spectacular blaze, highlighted by a raging snowstorm, on that February day in 1897 when this view was recorded for posterity.

Governor Hastings called it "a frightful mess," and he was not far from wrong. Harrisburg's second State Capitol was anything but an architectural masterpiece, as the above view emphasizes. The cornerstone was laid in 1898, and the building was opened for use in 1899, but never completed. This photo was taken about a year later.

In 1963 a man who had worked on the electrical installations stated emphatically that it was not razed, but stands enclosed in the present building. A comparison of various photographs taken during construction indicates his statement may be correct.

Patrice Gilnough, better known as "Paddy Gilner," although of humble lineage and profession, enjoyed the company of those who populated Capitol Hill around the turn of the century. He was a self-appointed, unpaid custodian of the main building. Every Christmas his politician friends dressed Paddy in holiday toggery and sent him forth rejoicing. Paddy, who was born in a little frame house on High Street, a long-vanished thoroughfare back of the old Capitol, died in 1916 at the age of sixty-eight.

Harrisburg's Federal Square, at Third and Walnut streets, began to take form in 1877 when old buildings were torn down to make way for a new post office. The accompanying photo was taken about two years later as the foundations were being constructed. The federal building was opened in 1887. Close inspection of the old photo reveals the slow, laborious methods necessary, and accounts for the long time between starting and finishing such a project.

The Dauphin County Bar Association was in session when this photo was taken in a courtroom of the old Court House on Market Street one day in 1890.

Those in the picture include Judges Simonton and McPherson, on the Bench. Among those seated are Murray Graydon, John Weiss, Samuel McCarroll (later a judge), M. W. Jacobs, L. M. Neiffer, Clayton Backenstow, Solomon Rupp, John E. Fox (later judge), and Isaac Swartz.

William Schooley models the approved attire for well-dressed members of the famous Harrisburg Wheel Club, while displaying his personal high-wheel bike of that day and generation.

The former mansion for the Commonwealth's governors, at Front Street and Barberry Alley, was actually two brick residences in 1864 when Governor Andrew Curtin moved in. A succession of alterations included the well-remembered brownstone facade, shown in this photograph, added at the insistence of Governor James A. Beaver in 1886. The history of the old mansion, razed just a few years ago, is a story in itself.

The sidewalks were brick, the street surface unpaved in this 1890s view of Second Street, looking north from State. Barely discernible are the street car tracks, proof of their existence being the two steel trolley-wire poles in the foreground. Many of the buildings in the photo are still there today in their original form.

About the turn of the present century this was how the old house at 210 Locust Street appeared. It was soon to be replaced by the New Lyceum Theater, and perhaps because of that fact Mr. James K. Dumars, who had been born there in 1845, chose to pose for the above picture with his son. The Dumars home and the other frame dwelling were soon to become but memories in the minds of older residents.

The other frame building, which stood at the corner of Locust and Court Streets, was to remain for several more years as the business place of Joseph Goldsmith, upholsterer.

In 1903 the New Lyceum Theater on Locust Street was opened to the public with great fanfare, featuring an initial performance by a large company headed by James T. Powers, a then popular comedian. Many prominent citizens were in attendance to hear Meade D. Detweiler, active in civic affairs of the day, formally present the play house to the residents of Pennsylvania's Capitol City. The Lyceum later was renamed The Orpheum and finally The State Theater, before being torn down in 1975 to make way for a modern office building.

"What this country needs is a good five-cent cigar"–Vice-President Thomas R. Marshall.

C. L. Boak, local cigar manufacturer, advertised his products in a unique manner. A racing sulky, driven by a clown, proclaimed the quality and price of "Knulls Ambrosia . . . Made in Harrisburg," as it toured the streets of the city.

Boys' High School class of 1882. Rear row, l. to r.: Frank B. Nickey, Milton M. Lemer, Elmer E. Saul, John K. Tomlinson (teacher), Frank Caum, and Lewis P. Crull. Front row: Daniel D. Hammelbaugh, James W. Miller, John Kurzenabe, J. Howard Wert (principal), George J. Kurzenabe, Clinton S. Mikle, and Warwick M. Ogelsby. Photo taken in front of the old Dewitt School on Walnut Street.

No. 6 North Market Square was about to become Samuel Kuhn's Clothing Store when this photo was taken in 1872. Next door at 6½, Miss Catherine Berryhill was the proprietor of a dry goods emporium. Note display of merchandise in the window. The Kuhn Clothing Company is no longer in business and, as of this writing, the site is now occupied by M. Lee Goldsmith Furniture Store.

E. A. Heffelfinger served residents of Allison's Hill from his "Triangle Grocery" at 1233 Derry Street in the 1880s. The proprietor has apparently just received a shipment of merchandise as witness the assortment of boxes and barrels in front of his establishment.

The corner of Third and Market streets being convenient to travelers ever since the first stage coach came to John Harris' village, it was a natural site for an inn. The first one there carried the Harris name. The second was the Lochiel, erected in 1868-69, pictured here. After a long and useful life it was sold to Wilmer & Vincent, theatrical promoters, who transformed it into the Colonial Theater, still operating at the same location as of 1975.

All played out. Teeners of the '90s had their musical groups too and practicing was tedious at times. On a hot afternoon in August, 1893, Ellen Kelker (guitar), Alice Graydon (mandolin), and Katherine Kelker relax on the rear doorstep of the H. A. Kelker residence, 25 South Second Street.

Five prominent Harrisburg families are represented in the group of young girls who posed for the accompanying photo, October 3, 1885:

Sara McConkey (blonde curls), Ellen and Edith Kelker, Mary Reily, and Florence Orth.

Ellen Kelker married A. Boyd Hamilton, local newspaperman, historian, and onetime legislative secretary. Her sister Edith married John Moffit. Descendants of all these families still reside in the city.

Railroading was a profession, not just another job, for many thousands of Harrisburg men years ago. Pride in their work and equipment is evidenced in this 1881 photo of a Philadelphia & Reading switching crew in the Harrisburg yards.

In the photo, l. to r., are: Horace Leeser, (brakeman), Herman Beard (fireman), Edward Geary (conductor), Charles Jones (engineman), Augustus Dewalt (brakeman), and William McFadden (brakeman).

The literary interests of local residents were served for many years by the State Library, the Methodist Reading Room, and the book stores of John Wyeth, George Bergner, and Philip German. In 1895, however, through the sponsorship of James McCormick, the Harrisburg Public Library opened its doors at 125 Locust Street, the location shown in the accompanying photograph.

There it remained until the move to the present stone structure at Front and Walnut streets took place. Further expansion later took place with the acquisition of the James McCormick home just across the street from the main building.

A tent city occupied the bluffs on the opposite side of the river from Harrisburg in June, 1863. According to Robert Grant Crist, Camp Hill, local historian who authored a monograph titled "Confederate Invasion of the West Shore–1863," the tents in this photo were occupied by troops of the New York National Guard that had been assigned to defend the state capital.

They manned a hastily-prepared fortification, named Fort Washington by General Darius N. Couch, in charge of Harrisburg's defense. The good general's name is perpetuated in history by another existing earthworks lying a short distance west of the main fort. Both locations are identified by historical markers.

The city's first public hospital was opened May 1873 in a small school building, which appears to the right of the righthand tree in this illustration. It was later joined to the main structure, which was dedicated February 22, 1884.

That building later was dwarfed by many extensions and additions that finally brought about its demise early in 1976. It was conveniently located adjacent to the tracks of the Cumberland Valley Railroad, later the Pennsylvania Railroad, and many a patient arrived at its doors via a special train consisting of a locomotive and caboose acting as an ambulance.

Other patients were brought in by a horse-drawn vehicle that was said to have served as an Army ambulance during the Civil War.

James McCormick's Paxton Furnaces were located on the family estate in south Harrisburg. Later the iron works were incorporated into the Chesapeake Nail Works and the Central Iron & Steel Company. Pictured in this photograph is one of the early industrial plant locomotives and its crew. Today all vestiges of the big steel mill complex have disappeared, torn down several years ago to make way for a planned industrial site.

Recreational facilities are nothing new to Harrisburg. At the turn of the century the city had already established a public park and bathing beach on Independence Island near the northern municipal limits. A spacious bathhouse and picnic pavilion (above) accommodated many hundreds of residents and their families on hot summer days long ago.

There were only two ways to get to Independence Island—by rowboat or the rope ferry shown in the accompanying photograph. Powered only by the river current, the large flat was secured in its course by a long cable stretched between the east shore of the river and the island. Two ropes with pulleys attached to either end of the craft kept it at an angle, and the flowing water propelled it on its journey.

Chapter 9

The Twentieth-Century City

Harrisburg in 1900 was in much the same state as that of a man who is aware of many personal lacks and shortcomings, but is uncertain just where and how to begin to correct them. To Myra Lloyd Dock goes the distinction of persuading city leaders to take the first step in the direction of improvement. Her address to the Board of Trade on December 20, 1900, prompted the employment of experts to survey the city's needs, the raising of a working fund, and the formation of the Municipal League. With the election of Vance C. McCormick as mayor in 1902, a program of improvement began with the construction of a water filtration plant on the island and a sewer to handle the effluent that for years had been polluting Paxton Creek and making the neighborhood both malodorous and unhealthy.

In 1902 another flood struck the city. In the same year the Market Street subway was opened for traffic although work was not completed on it until the next year. In 1904 came another flood and, oddly enough, the opening of another subway, the Herr Street underpass.

Old Home Week was observed during the first week of October, 1905, when the city greeted 25,000 ex-Harrisburgers and visitors with speeches and parades, festoons of electric lights and Chinese lanterns, and columns and arches in the streets and the Square.

The same year saw the completion of the widened Market Street bridge. This bridge was the first in the United States to boast a formal, dignified entrance. This was made possible through the generous gift of the Henry McCormick estate, which paid for the removal of the toll house and the erection of pillars from the old Capitol building. This entrance was dedicated on April 20, 1906.

To make the subway tally complete: the Paxtang subway under the P & R tracks was completed in time for the first trolleys to use it on May 30, 1906. It was Decoration Day then; there were still Civil War veterans to march to cemeteries and place flowers and flags on the graves of fallen comrades.

Two new theaters went up at this time: the Lyceum (in 1905) at Locust Street between Second and Third, and the Majestic (in 1907) at Walnut between Third and Fourth. Older citizens will remember the Lyceum as the Orpheum and later the State. In its palmy days the Orpheum presented many fine plays, ballets, and recitals by famous entertainers. A sampling includes Otis Skinner in *Kismet*, Pavlova, the Ballet Russe, Sir Harry Lauder, and Fritz Kreisler. It was there that Harrisburgers first saw the epic *Birth of a Nation* and Drinkwater's great *Abraham Lincoln*. And there for at least one summer were offered the weekly plays of a talented stock company. The Majestic was primarily a vaudeville theater, though in its later years it also presented stock.

The year that saw the birth of the Majestic also saw the destruction of one of the prides of Harrisburg—the Grand Opera House at Third and Walnut. On February 1 fire completely gutted that great building; it was never rebuilt.

But the great event of the first decade was the completion of the new Capitol. Within a few months after the burning of the old Capitol, plans were made for a new building, and the cornerstone was laid August 10, 1898. The new brick structure, however, pleased no one and in 1901 Senator John E. Fox introduced a bill providing for a new $4 million structure to supplant it. Governor William A. Stone signed the bill July 18, 1901, and on May 5, 1905 a new cornerstone was laid (just to the right of the main entrance).

Work progressed rapidly, and October 4, 1906 was selected as the dedication day. President Theodore Roosevelt accepted the invitation to make the dedicatory address. Thousands thronged the city (one estimate put the visitors at 80,000), streets and buildings were gay with bunting, flags, and strings of electric lights, and a large grandstand was erected on the west side of the Capitol grounds, facing the main entrance. Unfortunately, the weather did not cooperate; rain began in the early afternoon and continued through the rest of the day, but the dedication ceremony had been completed by that time: presentation of the Capitol to the Commonwealth by the Building Commission president, William A. Stone; acceptance by Governor Samuel W. Pennypacker; the main address by President Roosevelt, and the benediction by Bishop James H. Darlington.

In sheer magnificence Pennsylvania's Capitol is comparable only to the nation's Capitol. President Roosevelt called it the finest capitol in the nation.

The graft scandal which came later regarding the furnishings had nothing to do with their quality.

As might have been expected, the massive, majestic beauty of the Capitol challenged Harrisburg to renewed efforts to make the city a worthy setting. Through the years the parks grew more extensive and beautiful. Front Street Park and its river steps have become a showplace, as has Italian Lake Park, especially in the spring. Capitol Park, with its variety of trees, flowering shrubs, monuments, and statues is a delight to visitors. Reservoir Park, with its magnificent view, is a perennial favorite. It was the scene for many years of the annual Kunkel-sponsored Romper Day, when children took it over for a day of games, with refreshments served at long tables set out in the open.

Only Wildwood Park, carved out of what was once Wetzel's Swamp, has been neglected. But there are signs that it may stage a comeback. With the establishment there of the Harrisburg Area Community College Harrisburgers are taking a fresh look at the area. Birdwatchers and plant lovers still find it a minor paradise.

The riverfront has had a prominent place in Harrisburg life since the first days of John Harris' trading post. It has a history of its own from the boisterous "Hardscrabble" times to the early 1900s when Harry Berrier's and A. P. Dintaman's boathouses catered to the city's nautically inclined. But it was not until the second decade of the century that the city began at last to do something to curb the damage caused by the floods that often rose to fill basements and damage property along Front Street. Construction was commenced on the stepped riverbank retaining wall and the walkway that became a favorite promenade for strollers.

Many can still remember the coal barges that only a few decades ago dotted the river's surface opposite Harrisburg, dredging up the fine coal washed down from exposed seams in the coal region to the north. And hundreds of Harrisburgers can recall the annual grammar school track meets and later high school football and baseball games on the track and athletic fields in Island Park.

And today there is Harrisburg's Kipona, the unique late-summer river festival that through the years since it was first held on September 4, 1916 has given pleasure to thousands. Not everyone knows that Kipona is the brain-child of Edward J. Stackpole, lieutenant general, publisher, author, and humanitarian.

Harrisburg has always been blessed with civic-minded citizens who have initiated movements or contributed not only money but time to projects for the city's betterment. It is only fair to mention some of them who were prominent during the period covered in this chapter. The community owes much—to name just a few—to the Foxes, Gilberts, Hamiltons, Gorgases, McCormicks, Camerons, Stackpoles, McFarlands, and Kunkels.

For a random example, consider J. Horace McFarland. Founder of the McFarland Press and one of the nation's outstanding flower experts (particularly roses), he was instrumental in the establishment of the Sunken Garden (or Rose Garden) along Third Street near Division. It is now gone, a victim of the inevitable expansion of the splendid Polyclinic Hospital, but Giuseppe Donato's controversial *Dance of Eternal Spring* that had graced the center of the garden was moved (1971) to Italian Lake Park.

Harrisburg streets in the 1900s to 1920 presented—by today's standards—a quiet, almost deserted appearance. The horse still had his day, pulling drays, milk wagons, ice carts, buggies, and carriages, but the automobile was rapidly replacing him and gasoline pumps were no longer a curbside novelty. But parking meters were not yet even a dream in the inventor's mind.

Those were relatively leisurely days. One used the street cars or walked to one's destination: a business appointment, shopping "downtown," Saturday marketing, or a social call. Without radio or television families found means of entertainment in games and reading, occasional visits to the "movies," or parties and picnics.

And then came World War I. Those were the hectic days of Liberty Loan drives, always oversubscribed; the gasolineless Sundays; the recruiting, Red Cross, Liberty Bond, food conservation, and other colorful patriotic posters that filled the windows of stores and vacant buildings—posters that are now collectors' treasures— the windows of homes proudly displaying service flags with a star for each man in the service; the anxious daily scanning of the newspapers with their two-inch-high headlines; and the streets thronged at night with men from the nearby Army and Army Air Corps bases at Middletown and New Cumberland. Finally came the delirious excitement of November 11, 1918, when news of the Armistice closed schools and businesses to jam the downtown streets with singing, cheering civilians and soldiers.

The close of the conflict brought a temporary end to the war-born prosperity of the area's steel plants and other industries supplying war materiel. It also marked the end of an era. When Harrisburg moved into the 1920s, it was at an accelerated pace.

Flood waters in the spring of 1902 effectively put an end to the use of a covered bridge at Market Street. As a result of the pictured damage of the eastern span, a new steel bridge was built, and the remaining original section razed after surviving nearly a century of storms and floods.

It was a cold, damp October fourth in 1906. Harrisburg had prepared for a big celebration to mark the dedication of the new State Capitol building, but the weather appreciably reduced the size of the crowd gathered to hear President Theodore Roosevelt make the dedicatory address. Umbrellas were prevalent and the bunting dripped, but tough old Teddy stood bareheaded during the ceremonies, with no public address system to assist his presentation.

The writing machine business, like the computer business today, was expanding in 1901, and Harrisburg—growing industrially—became the headquarters of the Keystone Typewriter Company, a subsidiary of Elliott-Hatch, Inc. A former flour mill, on South Cameron Street opposite the entrance to the Cameron estate, served as office and factory. The firm later expanded and became the Elliott-Fisher Company, which about thirty years ago moved its operations to New England, leaving the former busy plant vacant.

145

Typical of a successful small businessman of his day and generation was Mr. A. P. Dintaman, who operated a flourishing boat livery in the 1100 block of North Front Street. The portrait was made by William Stoey.

One of the many business-sponsored displays featured in Harrisburg's Old Home Week Industrial Day parade, October 5, 1905, was the eight-horse float of Burns & Co. The teamsters were dressed in English "Beefeater" attire, but the display was of a patriotic nature. "Miss Liberty" and "Betsy Ross" were attended by a soldier and a sailor. An Indian chief in white also rode along to complete the scene.

Burns & Company, suppliers of home furnishings, did business for more than half a century at the same site on South Second Street, before a fire ended their existence several years ago.

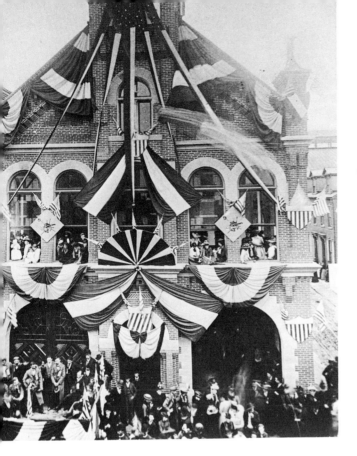

Gaily decorated Friendship Fire House, Third and Cherry, apparently served as a focal point for Harrisburg's Old Home Week celebration, October 1 to 7, 1905. Note the crowd around the reviewing stands in front of the building. The fire company was one of the city's oldest, having been organized prior to 1801. Friendship lost its home in recent years due to the redevelopment program in that area.

Dr. Ezra S. Meals and a friend pose in front of the ex-mayor's decorated property, Third and North streets, during Old Home Week.

A crowd of spectators gathered around J. B. Montgomery's float as it paused in Market Square while participating in the city's Industrial Day parade, a part of the Old Home Week celebration. The sight of two husky men screening coal atop a moving wagon probably elicited remarks among the onlookers.

It was a cold, dreary February 1, 1907, and the ruins of Harrisburg's famed Grand Opera House still smoldered while crowds of curious citizens gathered to view the results of a flash fire. Note the telephone repairman high on a pole at the corner of Walnut and Third, braving the elements to restore service. Almost a decade would pass before another building—the Penn-Harris Hotel—would rise on the same site. Now, it too is gone.

The Philadelphia & Reading Railway Company built its second passenger station at Harrisburg in the 1880s. It was a rambling structure north of Market Street, along the old canal. In this view a subway had replaced the former dangerous grade crossing and a new and larger station was planned for the opposite side of the street. That, too, disappeared to make way for the city's main Post Office.

Front, l. to r.: Jack Davis, Jerome Lewis, Oscar Beamer, Harry Bricker, Rudolph Bell, William Shindler, Ross Huber, Oscar Herman (conductor), A. B. Cleckner (yardmaster), Chas. Hess, Harry Rupert, Edward Rhodes, and W. J. Spangler.

Second Row: George Deimler, Jack Ambrosia, William Wright, John Holtzman, George Durbrow, William Wilson, George Ward, Edward Ebersole, Frank Mordan, Arthur Wager, Clarence Miller, and Ross Fasick.

On the engines: Jame Gary, Lyman Coldren, and Roy Porter.   *The date–1912.*

The Reading Company's big freight classification yard at Rutherford, just east of the city, has always been a busy spot. Sixty-three years ago the East Hump Night Trick Crew (in railroad lingo shifts are called "tricks") gathered for a group photo at the end of their tour of duty.

Because of its proximity to tobacco-producing Lancaster County, Harrisburg at one time boasted a dozen or more cigar factories. Some were small operations, others quite large. Workers in the C. L. Boak factory at 1221 North Third Street are pictured in this photograph.

An Early Taxi used in Harrisburg about 1901

Harrisburg's first motor-driven cabs were fancy affairs built to resemble rather closely the old horse-powered ones. Not further identified, if this one did actually run on the city streets, it probably would have been operated by the former Harrisburg Taxi and Baggage Company.

150

Vaudeville and minstrel shows were popular forms of entertainment during the early years of this century and many of the younger generation became "stage struck." Such was the case with the teenage daughters of Mr. and Mrs. John B. Malseed, 564 Race Street. Here they pose for the photographer during a rehearsal of one of their acts. The year: 1907.

At the turn of the century Jos. Claster was already a prominent merchant. The Claster emporium, located in a long-vanished brick building on the southeast corner of Second and Chestnut, moved to other locations in later years. A few doors to the left of the Claster store in this photograph can be seen the old Chestnut Street Market House. The trolley tracks in the foreground were those of the Race and Vine Street line.

In 1910 when this photo was taken the Pennsylvania Railroad employed more than 8000 men and women in the Harrisburg area. Servicing locomotives took a lot of work and a lot of workmen. This is much in evidence by the almost completely covered Class H-8 freight engine. J. A. Ringland (front row, holding derby) was enginehouse foreman at the time, a responsible position in those days.

This dip in the roadway on City Island between the east and west spans of the Market Street Bridge was filled in about forty years ago. Note the dust being stirred up by the traffic and the gas lamps to illuminate the walkway at night–back in the "days of yore"–1904.

The Wright Brothers' experiment stirred the imagination of many would-be inventors including J. W. Roshon, a local photographer. Roshon designed and built the odd contraption pictured here in 1909. His plane did not fly, because of the short runway erected on a lot at Fifth and Vaughn streets. Later, equipped with an 8 hp motor and tested from a bluff in Riverside, it again failed to take to the wide blue yonder, thus ending the Roshon experiment.

Harrisburg started its first grade-separation program in 1901 when workers began excavating for the Market Street subway. The reason, then as today, was increasing traffic and a number of fatal accidents on the old grade crossing.

The sign partially hidden by a telephone pole proclaims "Harrisburg's First Sky-Scraper. A modern eight-story bank and office building being erected on this site by Payne & Co. for the Union Trust Company." Date on photo, October 10, 1905. Building opened for use in June, 1906. Cost: $102,000 and still in use today on the northwest corner of Market Square.

A favorite ride for young members of the Harrisburg Wheel Club at the turn of the century was up the river to Rockville and return along the old canal towpath. No trip was complete without a stop at the Susquehanna Hotel, which stood along the river at Coxestown. The pump on the front porch provided cool water for those too young to obtain refreshment inside. The only identified member is Fred Morganthaler, with hands on hips.

It was July 4, 1907, and to celebrate the holiday Mr. and Mrs. A. Boyd Hamilton took their young son, the late Henry Kelker Hamilton, to River Park for an outing with Mr. Hamilton's grandfather, Dr. Hugh Hamilton, a prominent local physician.

No such thing as a special "rec" room in city homes years ago. Social events such as the corn-popping party shown here were often held in the parlor, if it boasted a fireplace. Those participating included, l. to r., Mary Pilkay, a teacher, and William Walters. In front of the fireplace, Bess Long, the hostess with back turned; Sara Walzer, and Bertha Sieber. Miss Pilkay was later killed when struck by an auto at Front and Broad streets.

Members of the Harrisburg School Board and administrators pose for a group photograph in 1910 in front of the district's headquarters on Chestnut Street.

L. to r., first row: Harry Leonard, William Boll, Edw. McKee, Harry Boyer, president, Dr. C. E. McKeen, Benjamin D. Boggs, and George W. Kennedy, truant officer. Second row: William Machlan, Dan M. Barr, Edw. Moeslein, Cameron L. Bair, and Dr. William Hughes. Third row: Daniel Hammelbaugh, secretary; Frank C. Sites, John Saul, John W. Urban, George W. Stachell. Fourth row: Charles F. Fohl, Clarence Cless, next three unidentified, John Williams, Simon Page, F. E. Downs, superintendent. Fifth row: First two unidentified, Frank Foose, and Austin Miller.

A mouth-watering display of candy Easter eggs, chocolate rabbits, and fancy baskets, topped by a miniature State Capitol building modeled in sugar, drew customers into the Sugar Bowl Confectionery at Third and Herr streets back in 1907. Note the reflection of the "Day and Night" chewing tobacco sign backlighting the ice cream soda advertisement on the window.

Harry Berrier's boatyard along the river, near Front and Herr streets, employed a big hand operated crane to move boats to and from the water in the early 1900s. Note the sand or coal flatboat under construction in the foreground, and the motorboat suspended by the crane.

Charles L. Boak, local cigar manufacturer, and Mrs. Boak pose for a portrait in the garden of their home on a sunny day in 1908. Fancy hats and high-necked blouses together with street-sweeping skirts were quite the fashion among the ladies in those days. No candy-striped blazer and white pants for Mr. Boak, who apparently preferred a more conservative attire.

City officials early recognized the need for recreational facilities. A floating bathhouse was constructed and anchored at the lower end of City Island in 1907. Previous facilities on Independence Island had been abandoned because of inaccessibility. Here the riverbottom was good for bathing and the water deep enough for swimming. Patronage was good, as evidenced in the photo.

Pennsylvania Canal boat no. 317 had made its last revenue trip. Tied up at Speeceville at the turn of the century, it waited scrapping. Water in this section of the "big ditch" remained until the flood of 1903 caused it to drain away, leaving abandoned boats high and dry.

The winter of 1902-03 was one with plenty of snow, as indicated in this scene along North Front Street, above Herr. People shoveled the white stuff into the street (just as they do today). But then it lay until the sun or rain took it away—no such things as front-end loaders, plows, and trucks in those days. Floundering horses, pulling sleighs and delivery sleds, gradually worked their way through the accumulation to eventually create a passable thoroughfare. Note that there are buildings on both sides of Front Street in this photograph. The buildings on the river side of Front Street were removed in the early twenties to make way for the extension of River Park.

A coal and sand dredge works in the east channel of the river, opposite Front and Hamilton streets in 1902. Several fleets of these craft worked the riverbed here for many years, providing much local employment and boosting the city's economy.

There was still water in the bed of the canal north of Dauphin in 1900. Above the abandoned waterway a Northern Central passenger train steams towards Harrisburg with an official business car on the rear end.

After a cruise on the river in one of Harry Berrier's boats or canoes, patrons were tempted to pause in his handy ice cream parlor. The young waitress apparently was ready to serve the photographer on that bright day back in 1907. Potted plants, flowers on the tables, and even electric lights created an atmosphere of relaxation. Homemade lampshades of oiled paper hung from the ceiling. The streamers were of crepe. Paper lampshades were practical in those days since electric light bulbs did not generate enough heat to constitute a fire hazard.

Advertisement for A. P. Dintaman's Boat Livery (1909-1920).

Sidewheelers were not common among the craft on the Susquehanna at Harrisburg. To have something different, Andrew Sullenberger built the Ella C, *shown in this 1905 picture taken opposite Independence Island. The paddle wheels were manually operated by hand cranks. Captain Sullenberger and crew relax for a moment while the photographer goes about his task.*

Harrisburg's riverfront was cluttered with coal flats, boat docks, and unsightly fill in 1903 before the Harrisburg Telegraph *mounted a beautification campaign. This view is looking upstream from the foot of Forster Street. In the distance can be seen the West Fairview-Harrisburg ferry* Kingfisher *approaching the east shore.*

One of the many attractions featured on the stage of the old Grand Opera House was The Seminary Girls, *with 74 people in the cast, as advertised on one of Dr. J. H. Fager's billboards, located along South Cameron Street in 1901.*

In 1903 the Pennsylvania Railroad constructed the then largest freight classification yard in the United States across the river from Harrisburg in Enola. Hills were leveled in the process, and here we see one of the contractor's "dinky" engines pulling a string of dump cars loaded with fill from a huge steam shovel.

"Any ice today, lady?" The United Ice & Coal Co. and H. A. E. Walkemeyer competed for the food preservation business in Harrisburg in the early 1900s. Here is one of United's big wagons pausing to deliver a cake of ice to a private home on South Front Street.

What the well-uniformed Harrisburg police officer wore in the early 1900s is modeled by Captain Backenstoss, who posed for the above portrait in the mayor's office one day long ago.

South Second Street looking north from about Washington before the railroad overpass was constructed. A close look will reveal the crossing gates and watchman's shanty to the right, behind the horse and buggy. A trolley trundles south to Race and Vine streets while a canopied touring car chugs north towards Chestnut Street and Market Square. The steeple of the Market Square Presbyterian Church and the top story of the newly completed Union Trust Building vie for prominence in the background.

Suburbia was beginning to spread in the early years of the twentieth century. Evidence of this shows in this 1905 view of Lemoyne (formerly Riverton). Looking south from the hill topped by Fort Washington of Civil War vintage, the camera takes in the buildings along Market Street, the Cumberland Valley Railroad yards, E. K. Frazer's lumber mill, and a growing number of private homes.

The river coal and sand business required transfer from flatboats to vehicles such as the two-wheel dump carts owned and operated by Cyrus Weidel, 1108 North Front Street, pictured here. The transfer point was below Dintaman's boathouse, with nary a motor truck in sight. Note the two swimmers near the paddle wheel of the steamboat.

The Penn-Central's big freight yards at Enola have served the Harrisburg area for more than three-quarters of a century. This is how they looked just a few years after completion in 1903. Shadows indicate an early morning hour when the photographer pointed his camera north towards the gap at Rockville to record a scene of activity on the onetime "Standard Railroad of the World."

Streets and highways for the most part were unpaved. Automobiles were in the experimental stage and horsepower in the flesh, instead of under the hood, provided propulsion for over-the-road vehicles. J. R. Baker's Carriage and Wagon Works, Lemoyne, built a variety of such, as indicated by this photo taken about a decade before the factory was destroyed by fire in 1912.

Ferry service across the Susquehanna in the immediate vicinity of Harrisburg continued intermittently from the early 1700s over a period of about 200 years. One of the routes which survived until the 1920s was between New Cumberland and Steelton. In this 1908 picture the ferryboat is tied up at the West Shore landing. Note the coal barges nearby.

A double-headed Baltimore-Harrisburg Pennsylvania Railroad passenger train heads towards the city from the West Shore via the old Cumberland Valley Railroad Bridge amidst smoke and steam on a day in 1907. Note the low water in the river and the tracks of the "low grade" freight line from Enola to the east in the foreground.

Open-air trolley cars were quite the fashion during the early 1900s, especially on hot summer days. The Harrisburg Traction Company operated many like the one shown above with its proud crew awaiting passengers at Sixth and Camp streets years ago.

The Pennsylvania Railroad's operations here were so large at the beginning of the twentieth century that two roundhouses were required to service the many locomotives. Supervisory force at No. 2 enginehouse consisted of W. C. Bickley, foreman (in the window), and E. M. Croll, F. A. Kaufman, A. A. Poist, W. C. Church, and Frank Hall. The date–1908.

Posing on the unfinished front steps of the present Capitol Building in 1904 were a group of local painters employed in putting the finishing touches to the handsome edifice. The men in the front row are apparently officials and supervisors. The only man to be identified in the group was Samuel Bear, of Lemoyne, standing in the rear row, fourth from the left. (Photo courtesy of Miss Miriam Bear, Lemoyne)

The Pennsylvania Railroad's famous stone arch bridge, eight miles north of the Capitol, had just been completed when this picture was taken in 1902. Construction crews had turned their attention to the task of removing the old span, thus changing the view across the Susquehanna, looking eastward from the West Shore.

Young girls and their dolls are still in style, just as they were back in 1903 when Miss Mary Stape sat for her portrait in her own backyard, looking as pretty as the flowers which serve as a background.

Pennsylvania's governor, Martin G. Brumbaugh, demonstrated his ability to handle a team of horses during the observance of "Good Roads Day," May 16, 1916. The good governor participated in ceremonies held between Millersburg and Halifax on what is now Route 15.

Proof that "women power" existed sixty years ago is indicated in the picture. The ladies are all from Halifax and Millersburg and they are taking part in the observance of a statewide "Good Roads Day" program. Here they "work" on a stretch of highway that is now a part of Route 15, under the direction of Gov. Martin G. Brumbaugh, who made the occasion an official one.

Sitting l. to r.: Ralph L. (Boney) Miller, "Si" Boob, and Charles (Cholly) Grier, all members of the South Harrisburg Amusement Company that flourished about 1915. They performed mostly at local fairs and festivals.

The northwest corner of Fourth and Market streets looked quite different in 1909 from its appearance today. Pomeroy's department store is still there, but in a much altered form. Dives and Stewart have not been associated with the store name for quite a few years now. Note the chinaware in the glass case on the front of the small brick building that once housed the offices of the Adams Express Company.

An unexpected thrill for crowds watching Harrisburg's first air show was added when one of the three primitive airplanes crashed in Paxtang Park. An early barnstorming group of aviators, led by Paul Peck of Washington, D.C., put on the show using a farmer's field bordering Derry Street. No serious injuries were sustained by the pilot of the ill-fated plane, but crowds of curious spectators swamped the Harrisburg Traction Company's cars and the park facilities.

The first widening of the Lemoyne bottleneck got under way in 1909 when the Pennsylvania Highway Department approved a contract for the job. Note the "water boy" with his buckets, the horse-powered dump cart, and the men on the hillside getting ready to blast the rock formation. On the right is the coal yard and stable of the Paxton Flour and Feed Company, now the location of Shaull's, Inc.

The capital city of the Keystone State has many distinctions, one of which is the proximity of the longest stone arch railroad bridge in the world (3792 feet). Cost of construction was $2,100,000. It was put into service April 1, 1902, when the first eastbound passenger train, shown in the photo, was greeted by railroad officials and representatives of the contractors.

When The Birth of a Nation *played for the first time at the old Orpheum on Locust Street, this was the front page of the program that the Wilmer & Vincent Theatre Company, managers of the theater, passed out to each customer.*

The messenger boys of yesteryear were seen at all times, day and night, rain or shine, in any part of the city, busy at the task of delivering telegrams for the Western Union and the Postal Telegraph companies.

One day in 1908 a group of Western Union boys paused for their picture in Market Square. First on the left, in the front row, is Joseph A. Snow, now in his eighties and still living in Camp Hill. Standing at the rear of the group is Earl Aurand, who lost his life in World War I and is memorialized through a veterans' post named for him.

In the early morning hours of May 11, 1905 local citizens were aroused by a tremendous explosion. A westbound Pennsylvania Railroad passenger train, the Cleveland Express, had collided with a freight train carrying a carload of dynamite. The wreck occurred at Lochiel, between Steelton and the city limits. Twenty-two persons lost their lives and 136 were injured. Some of the victims were interred in a common grave located in Paxtang Cemetery.

The accompanying picture was taken after daylight as wrecking cranes were busy at the task of cleaning up the mess. The locomotive is that of the Cleveland Express.

Miss Naomi Miller and her niece enjoy a few quiet moments in the backyard of her home on a balmy spring day in 1898. The young girl with her doll and the young lady with her book combine to accentuate the average pace of life in those far-off days.

175

The explosion caused by the tragic Lochiel train wreck shattered windows in factories, business places, and homes over a wide area of south Harrisburg. Practically every window of the Elliott-Hatch typewriter factory nearby was broken by the big blast.

A typical family parlor in the 1890s was that of the B. I. Lingle family, 312 Boas Street. Mr. Lingle was a local painting contractor. Note the knickknack shelf on the back wall, the heavily framed pictures hanging nearby. A rococo oil lamp with a naked cupid stands on the parlor table together with family photos. Dark curtains frame the doorway to the next room, matching the attire of the family group. Everyone seems to be occupied at the moment except the family dog who keeps a wary eye on the photographer.

In the heyday of steam railroading (1910) a courageous cameraman records thrilling action in the form of a speeding eastbound Pennsylvania Railroad passenger train along the Susquehanna River just below Steelton, heading for Philadelphia, or possibly New York, on a crisp winter day long ago.

Where in the world was the "Beelzebub" distillery? The only identification for this intriguing photograph in the Stoey collection was that and the date, September 1, 1901.

A turn-of-the-century view of parts of Harrisburg's Seventh and Eighth wards provides an interesting comparison with that of today. The photo was taken from the J. Ensminger property, located on Cumberland Street, looking southwest.

The houses in the foreground face Twelfth Street, in the block between Herr and Cumberland; the church to the right, the Bethany Presbyterian. To the left can be seen a portion of the

At one time Harrisburg boasted a ''Boys Brigade''–presumably when local patriotism ran high during the Spanish-American War. This picture, in the Stoey collection, was identified simply as ''Sullenberger's Boys on the Capitol steps'' and apparently was copied from an original by Le Rue Lemer, well-known professional photographer in the city years ago.

No date was given, but it must have been taken in the late 90s because the old Capitol burned in February 1897.

Harrisburg Pipe & Pipe Bending Company plant, while in the distance the tower of Central High School dwarfs the steeple of Messiah Lutheran Church. Near the center of the photo is the Ridge Avenue Methodist Episcopal Church and directly in front can be seen the Herr Street Bridge over the Pennsylvania Canal.

Whatever was the reason for this picture of Elmer E. Stoey, 645 Boas Street, and three of his fellow Knights Templar members has been lost in the mists of the passing years. Mr. Stoey is on the left. All that was noted on the back of the original print was the date, November 24, 1906, and "Elmer Stoey and chums."

Like many other business places in the city during World War I, the Harrisburg Light & Power Company provided window displays promoting the sale of Liberty Bonds. The offices of the company were located on North Second Street next to the Union Trust Building for many years.

Chapter 10

Harrisburg Between the Wars

The years between the two world wars were years of growth for Harrisburg. The booming new prosperity that followed the ending of World War I was evidenced in the city's rapidly changing appearance, as old buildings were torn down to make way for new, taller structures. Yearly the skyline of the city, viewed from the west shore of the river, grew more impressive.

But not all of the changes have been happy ones for tradition-minded Harrisburgers. There was a time when Front and State streets were the heart and mind of the city. There for a long time lived the "movers and shakers" of Harrisburg. The fine old houses that lined them were once the homes of everybody who was somebody—Harrisburg's "400." A list of the names would be a roster of those who led or strongly supported the activities that made Harrisburg what it is today. We will not attempt to name them all; a sampling is sufficient: Cameron, Maclay, Kunkel, Stackpole, Wickersham, Reily, Bailey, Gross, Doutrich, McCreath, Payne, McCormick, Hickok, Wharton, Gilbert, Fox, Hamilton, Boas, Detweiler, Royal, Tracy, Wallower.

Front Street, and State Street from Third to the river, like other sections of Harrisburg, have been victims of the changes that accompany "progress." Some houses have been torn down and replaced; others have been converted to offices and business establishments. Dutch elm disease has claimed the stately trees that once helped to make Front Street Harrisburg's pride. But enough of the old remains to make a tour of the district a rewarding experience for the antiquarian and casual tourist alike. Not too late, it is hoped, efforts are being made to preserve and restore something of the past. The Dauphin County Historical Society has done nobly in recording the city's early history. A hopeful sign is the recent organization of the Historic Harrisburg Association, which had its beginning in south Harrisburg. Here homeowners have lovingly restored and refurbished nineteenth-century houses, some of which are open on occasion for the Association's guided walking tours.

Perhaps the most notable of the changes came in the State Capitol complex. For years preceding the 20s the state government's departments and bureaus had been housed in office buildings scattered through the downtown section of the city. Now in rapid succession the North and South office buildings rose to add impressive grandeur to Capitol Hill, along with the Education Building, which includes the magnificent Forum and the State Library.

The school system, almost static for a generation, underwent rapid development. For many years Harrisburg had marked time with its grammar schools and the old Central (coed, 1893) and Technical (boys, 1904) high schools. There was intense athletic rivalry in both groups, particularly between Central and Tech. For years Central dominated (outstanding athletes were the well-remembered "Shorty" Miller and "Rabbit" Rote), but the rivalry ended when Central became the girls' high school. Tech went on to claim the national high school football championship in 1919, scoring 701 points to none against such opponents as Mercersburg Academy, Perkiomen Prep, and challengers from Cedar Rapids, Iowa and Portland, Maine. This team of all-stars (left halfback Carl Beck made Harrisburg famous in sports) was coached by local attorney Paul G. Smith.

Central and Tech closed their doors in 1926; on September 7 of that year the new William Penn High School ("uptown") received its first students and on the twentieth John Harris ("high upon the eastern hill") opened its doors to muddy-footed faculty and pupils; the sidewalks had not yet been paved. Dr. Charles Fager, beloved principal at old Tech, headed the William Penn faculty; Walter E. Severance went to John Harris from Central. In football, John Harris continued the Tech tradition with undefeated teams in 1929-1931. Scholarship was not neglected; both schools graduated excellent scholars.

In 1930 a third high school opened, Bishop McDevitt Catholic High, also on "the hill" at Market and Twenty-second streets. It promptly entered into the intracity scholastic and athletic rivalry.

It is an interesting sidelight that attendance at old Tech engendered a loyalty that found fruition in the formation of the Tech Golden Legion in 1928. In June each year graduates meet for a day at Allenberry on the Yellow Breeches Creek to renew old acquaintance and indulge in orgies of reminiscence. Loyal ex-Tech men come from as far away as California, Florida, and even outside the States. Each year a class is formally inducted into the Legion on its fiftieth graduation anniversary. The final induction will come in 1976, the nation's bicentennial year. The Tech Golden Legion is indeed a unique organization—another Harrisburg first.

Keeping pace with the material developments in the city, in a little more than the decade following the war Harrisburg saw the birth of the Art Association of Harrisburg and the Harrisburg Symphony Orchestra. The Art Association was founded in 1926 by a group of talented local artists: Harold Booth, Walt Huber, Earl Johnston, Nick Ruggieri, and Alden Turner. Its home is the old Executive Mansion of Governor Findlay (1817-1820) at 21 North Front Street. The Association's numerous exhibits of the work of local artists are convincing proof that artistic talent is no rarity in Harrisburg.

The Harrisburg Symphony Orchestra began its brilliant career in the William Penn High School auditorium on March 19, 1931 under the baton of George King Raudenbush. It has flourished since then and has attracted to its ranks outstanding local talent and gifted musicians from as far away as Lancaster. Its concerts are now held in the Forum.

Too many Harrisburgers have benefited from the services of our hospitals to omit at least mention of them. Dr. Hartman's hospital, the Keystone, at Third and Briggs is now only a memory. But the Harrisburg Hospital and the Polyclinic not only remain but are constantly expanding their facilities and their services, while two others have been added recently, The Osteopathic Hospital and Holy Spirit Hospital.

Harrisburg is nationally famous as the home of the Pennsylvania State Farm Show, held yearly during early January. For many years exhibitors were crowded into buildings in the downtown section; now a single great building at Cameron and Maclay streets provides extensive space for displays and a huge arena for animal judging and various farm-related contests. Here, too, is held the internationally acclaimed Horse Show, where contestants from all over the world meet to compete in equestrian skills.

Floods are part of the way of life in the capital, and its residents take all but the worst in stride. One of the "worsts" was the so-called Saint Patrick's Day flood of 1936.

The winter of 1935-1936 was a hard one in Pennsylvania, with heavy snowfall and weather so cold that there was little melting. Tire chains cut gullies in the city streets. Then came a thaw, beginning in late February, that overflowed the banks of every stream feeding into the Susquehanna, and the river came down like a tidal wave. The flood reached its peak at 6 P.M. on March 19, when south Harrisburg and Cameron Street went under water that crested at 30.33 feet.

What gave the flood its fearsome quality were the huge cakes of ice it carried—ice that battered down utility poles, houses, and bridges in its path. With the pumping station and the island filtering plant out of commission, Harrisburg eked out its scanty reservoir supply with the help of a fleet of tank trucks which oil companies and others generously furnished for water transport. For more than a week the city went bathless, rationing the water; for safety's sake all drinking water was boiled.

The property loss was enormous; cleanup crews worked into late spring hauling away mud and sludge and ruined household goods. But within the year Harrisburg had recovered, talk about the often-discussed river wall for south Harrisburg had subsided, and it was "business as usual."

One good thing came as a result of the

flood, however. In 1940 the city dedicated a dam in Clark Valley in the Stony Mountain–Peter's Mountain area. Named after Councilman William T. DeHart, it is capable of supplying Harrisburg with 16 million gallons of water every day. Within seven years pipeline construction was completed and use of water from the Susquehanna was discontinued. The DeHart Dam insured the city against any repetition of the 1936 water shortage. It was a wise precaution, although most citizens believed with Governor George Earle that no flood so disastrous could ever happen again. They were wrong, of course; the 1972 Agnes flood was far worse.

The late 1930s witnessed the transition from electric trolley cars to buses. One by one the various city trolley lines made their last runs as the rails were taken up or paved over, and by July, 1939 Harrisburg was traveling on the more versatile buses.

Harrisburg's onward march faltered and marked time when the stock market crashed in 1929 and the Great Depression numbed most business activities. Banks failed, businesses went under, and Harrisburg, along with the rest of the nation, looked desperately to Washington for a solution. President Franklin Roosevelt's alphabetical agencies brought some relief with make-work public projects; one can still see along the Paxtang Driveway the paths laboriously cut along the eastern hillside. But a return of real prosperity had to wait until after a new war in Europe, with the resultant postwar demand for goods.

For those who remembered the First World War, World War II was an entirely different matter. In the first, we spent a year enthusiastically "saving the world for democracy" and accepting almost light-heartedly the sacrifices it demanded; the second was a far grimmer four-year struggle to save ourselves. Between volunteering and the draft, almost every family had one or more members—men and women—in the armed services. We accepted gasoline rationing with its books of tiny "A" stamps entitling us to five gallons a week, and turned in our extra tires to combat the shortage brought about by the Japanese conquest of the rubber-producing countries. Harrisburgers lined up at their neighborhood school buildings to secure their food ration books; they turned in aluminum pots and pans to supply the metal to make the planes that were to help win the war, and they bought $25 government "E" bonds from their earnings.

V-E Day and then V-J Day finally came, and Harrisburg gratefully took up again the pursuits of peace. But as with the First World War, the second marked the end of an era. Yet if we may judge from the past, Harrisburg's future is bright.

The records of old Harrisburg are well worth preserving. In a book, *Pennsylvania Today,* written in 1962 for the State Department of Public Instruction, one of the authors of this volume stated for Pennsylvania a truth which applies equally to Harrisburg—or perhaps to any community: "What we are today rests its foundations upon what we were through all our yesterdays."

Hundreds of Harrisburgers have in their possession records of the city's yesterdays in the form of diaries, letters, photographs, and the like which ought to be preserved, in copies or originals, in some central repository for reference by future students and historians. The Dauphin County Historical Society and the Historic Harrisburg Association do what they can, but they are limited to what is brought to them or what members can discover. In attics and old trunks, and among cherished family records all over the city there must be much memorabilia that would fill out the picture of the Harrisburg that was.

Harrisburg has a proud history. Surely fuller knowledge of its past can only deepen its citizens' pride.

The skyline of the Commonwealth's capital city provides a backdrop for this unusual view of activity in connection with the construction of the present Market Street Bridge between City Island and Front Street. Cars carrying stone for the span were placed on an elevated spur from the Cumberland Valley Railroad bridge for unloading. A crane then transfered the blocks to flatboats to be floated to the pier sites.

Interest in youthful recreation and education was widely promoted by the local YMCA in years past. The boys' game room of the old "Y" Building at Second and Locust streets doubled as a classroom for Bible study. Here was one of the youthful classes, taught by Robert Hamer, a dedicated worker with boys during the period immediately following World War I.

Harrisburgers have always been sportsminded. Fifty years ago outdoor volleyball was in vogue and several leagues were playing on city and privately owned lots. On a summer day in 1926 teams from the Telegraph Press and Hickok Manufacturing Company played on a vacant lot bordering South Seventeenth Street. They, together with teams from the Kinney Shoe Company and Reading Railroad, also playing on the double court, were members of the Industrial Volleyball League, sponsored by the Harrisburg YMCA.

Since the days of John Harris, the city has been a site for the storage of military supplies. The first arsenal was erected on Capitol Hill in 1817. In 1874 it was removed to its present site at Eighteenth and Herr streets. In 1914 the entire structure with the exception of the tower was torn down and the present building erected. Following the destruction of the old Capitol by fire in 1897, the iron fence surrounding it was moved to the arsenal, where it remains today.

City dwellers took some pride in their property years ago, too, as indicated in the accompanying photograph of a residential backyard at the intersection of Derry Street with Market and Cameron. Trees, flowers, shrubbery, and grass added a touch of graciousness to the adjoining brick pavement and gravel roadway on a summer day in 1913.

Hard work and humor went together on the railroad years ago. In the early 20s the Pennsylvania Railroad No. 1 enginehouse hostlers and ash pit gang got together for this photograph, not forgetting their mascot "Nell."

Back row, l. to r.: unknown, Rex Winters, William Plant, Charles Gardner, next two unidentified. Second row, George Toomey, George Gardner, H. L. Burris, George Zeiders, unidentified. Front row, unidentified, Nell the mascot, and John Flick, hostler gang foreman.

The photographer apparently piqued the curiosity of several pedestrians as he opened the lens of his camera on Market Street near the Square on a chilly day in January, 1914. Others go their way unmolested by traffic while a Harrisburg Railways trolley waits for passengers. In the distance is a single automobile, parked near Front Street. Two police officers stand in the center of the Square ready to direct traffic—when it comes!

Frank S. Musser, president of the Harrisburg Railways Company and S. Shaul Rutherford, prominent local caterer, take time out to discuss the development of Camp Shikellimy for the Harrisburg YMCA on a fall day in 1920.

189

The entrance to the Commonwealth's Capitol gets a face-lifting in 1928. A wider approach, similar to that of the national Capitol in Washington, added a touch of elegance to the imposing structure.

A "Slow Keep Right" sign on the traffic signal in the foreground apparently was ignored by a careless driver.

On a warm summer day in 1922 it took four motor trucks plus a caterpillar tractor to haul just one of the huge granite pillars up State Street from the railroad to the site of the present South Office Building in the developing Capitol complex. At that time State Street extended from the rear of the Capitol eastward to and across the railroad at Seventh Street. Meanwhile a Sixth Street trolley waits the passing of the convoy of Central Storage Company equipment.

Redevelopment is nothing new to Harrisburg. It has been an almost unending process, as witness this May 19, 1919 view of that area of downtown lying southwest of the Capitol. Compared to earlier views published elsewhere in this book, the changes are instantly apparent.

Forerunner of today's Farm Show in Harrisburg was the Great Granger's Picnic held each summer at Williams Grove Park, nine miles west in the Cumberland Valley. To accommodate exhibitors and officials from out of town the rustic hotel pictured here was operated under the management of the late Charles Hoerner, Lemoyne, who afterwards became active in area Boy Scout work.

River traffic was heavy on Kipona Day, 1915. A police officer in a motorboat (center) watches as another craft heads towards an apparent collision with a flatboat while occupants of the canoe in the foreground look on. Note the converted coal scow, complete with seats and protective awning, to the right.

The old Eighth Ward, back of the Capitol, was disappearing as homes, churches, schools, and business places were being demolished in 1917 to make way for the start of the present Commonwealth complex. Looking east, all that remains today are the railroad yards and the buildings of the Harrisburg Steel Company. The Soldiers and Sailors Memorial Bridge and state office buildings now occupy the balance of the territory west of the railroad.

A Boy Scout uniform far different from today's is modeled by an unidentified young man about fifty years ago. Note the merit badges on his sleeve, the black cotton stockings, hiking shoes, canteen, and scout axe, which complete the outfit.

Typical of the neighborhood grocery stores in 1915 was that of Charles R. Low, located at the corner of Sixth and Herr streets. Evidently he was promoting the sale of Gosman's Ginger Ale, "Guaranteed to comply with the Pure Food and Drugs Act of 1906." Note the penny chewing gum vending machine at the extreme left. "Both phones" meant that Mr. Low had telephones of both the Bell system and the United Telephone Company. The United Telephone Company was and still is a competitor of the Bell Telephone Company. It maintains its headquarters in its own building near Carlisle. Today its services are coordinated with the area Bell system.

Pick and shovel and muscle did the job back in 1914 when the river wall was being constructed. The only machines in the picture are a cement mixer and the steam dredge in the distance. Location, near Front and Forster, where the Taylor Memorial Bridge is now.

Lemoyne station, formerly designated as Bridgeport by the Cumberland Valley Railroad, as it looked about half a century ago. It was here in the very early days of the railroad that weary stage coach passengers transferred to the first railroad sleeping car to operate in the United States to continue their journey as far as Chambersburg. The station shown here was built in 1893 and torn down about ten years ago to make way for expansion of the Shaull Equipment Company complex.

One of the first electrical equipment stores in Harrisburg was the Dauphin Electrical Supplies Company, 434 Market Street. The firm was headed by John S. Musser, a brother of Frank Musser, president of the local street railway.

Standing in the doorway of the store are, l. to r., Andrew Potts, Foster Sowers, Samuel Jones, and Robert Bailey. The date: 1915.

At one time the Pennsylvania and Reading railroads vied with the steel mills for employing the most local citizenry. This picture, a group photo of one shift of car shop workers and their supervisors at Enola in 1914, provides support for the railroads' claim. The railroads probably employed a total approximating 18,000.

The Porter family mansion at Front and Harris streets, built in the 1880s, was purchased by the Polyclinic Hospital January 1, 1915 and converted to medical use. The big old home served in this capacity until 1926, when the Polyclinic moved into the first unit of its present complex.

The Harrisburg Fire Department kept up with the times. Fire Chief Marion Verbeck and his assistant pose for a photographer in the department's 1915 model Overland roadster. Note the righthand drive, acetylene headlights, and coal oil cowl lamps. Accessories include a big brass bell and running board-mounted fire extinguisher.

Washington Hose Company No. 4 was located at a strategic spot downtown, on Chestnut Street between Front and Second. The Harrisburg Hospital's parking garage occupies the site today. This picture shows the "Washie's" two-horsepower chemical wagon ready to sally forth to fight a blaze. Note the horse blankets on the driver's seat and oil lamps mounted on each side.

One of the Harrisburg Fire Department's most impressive pieces of equipment years ago was the hook and ladder wagon of the Mount Vernon Hook and Ladder Company, then located on North Fourth Street, above Walnut. The large semicircular object mounted on the side of the vehicle is a folding net to catch fire victims jumping to safety during a blaze.

A 1916 Kipona boat parade entrant was Mooley Sheck. Apparently Mooley's family was quite proud of their decorated craft and obtained the services of photographer Stoey to record it all on film at Harry Berrier's boat yard.

Promenaders on Harrisburg's riverfront walk past the rear of John Yingst's store on North Front Street during the 1916 Kipona Day event. Numerous boats and canoes are visible in the distance, opposite the river steps that had been completed as far as Broad Street.

Some home brew and illegal liquor went into the gutter instead of stomachs during Prohibition days in Harrisburg. In this 1924 photo a U.S. deputy marshal (on right) supervises the operation. The illegal brew had been stored in a building about where the rear of the Lee store is today on North Third Street.

Harrisburg's City Hall, due to be replaced in the Harristown project, was at one time Harrisburg Technical High School, an all-boy seat of learning in 1923 when this view was taken. The rubble in the foreground came from demolished buildings of the old Eighth Ward. Today that vacant ground is part of the landscaping adjacent to the State Educational Building.

Safety on the highway was becoming an ever growing concern of the public and government alike in 1928. Here a member of the State Highway Patrol places a safety inspection sticker on Governor John S. Fine's big Lincoln sedan while the Governor, his chauffeur, and another officer look on. Passersby also pause to see what is going on.

Silhouetted against a night sky, Pennsylvania's State Capitol blazes with lights as the cleaning people go about their tasks. The temporary office buildings and the vacant ground testify of things to come. Only the South Office Building was up and in use when this 1925 photo was taken for Highway Department files.

Weatherbeaten and worn, the old covered bridge at Clark's Ferry on Route 22 north of Harrisburg had become inadequate for increasing highway traffic. In 1925, when this picture was taken, the ancient span was in the process of becoming history. A glimpse of the cement bridge that replaced it can be seen back of the tree at the bridge entrance.

Imagine the Lemoyne bottleneck without traffic! Well, it was when a Highway Department photographer set up his camera east of the twin railroad bridges on a day in 1928. Tracks of the Valley Railways still occupied a portion of the brick-paved right-of-way and a pathway on the side of the road was just plain dirt.

Jaywalking was "verboten" fifty years ago as illustrated here by the posted photograph of two young women holding up traffic while one looks for something in her purse, oblivious of the fact that she is surrounded by stalled autos, irate drivers, and an impatient police officer.

The location, Third and Walnut streets, a busy corner for many, many years.

One spring day in 1927 George Reist's Dance Boat was anchored just south of the Walnut Street Bridge on the west side of City Island in preparation for the coming season. For many years it was popular with young and old alike who danced to the tunes of famous bands on warm summer evenings long ago.

It is the summer of 1928 and the Capitol complex continues to grow. The North Office Building construction proceeds apace as the buildings in the city's old Eighth Ward continue to disappear into the photo files of history.

The gentleman in the black hat and wearing a clerical collar apparently was oblivious of the cameraman trying to take a picture of the temporary office buildings under construction at the rear of the main Capitol building. The trolley tracks serving the Sixth Street and Capital Street lines had been relocated from an abandoned stretch of Sixth Street to Commonwealth Avenue.

Pennsylvania's Governor Gifford Pinchot, an ardent outdoorsman and no stranger to the saddle, salutes parade watchers as he rides down Pennsylvania Avenue in Washington, D.C. on the occasion of President Calvin Coolidge's inauguration, March 4, 1925.

In 1933, following approval of the Twentieth Amendment to the Constitution, the inauguration date was advanced to January 20.

In addition to coal, the riverbed in the Harrisburg area was an important source of sand for local contractors. A truck belonging to John A. Albright is parked at the water's edge of the west bank between the Market and Walnut Street bridges in this 1927 view. The photograph is looking south from the Walnut Street Bridge. An electric conveyor dumps sand being shoveled from the barge into the truck. Note the extended piers of the Market Street Bridge awaiting use. The arched bridge in the background is the present Penn-Central Railroad bridge, formerly the Cumberland Valley Railroad bridge.

The thrill of flying, be it model airplanes or kites, still absorbs the interest of youth as it did thirty or more years ago when Richard Herman and Robert Cobaugh viewed models on display at a YMCA-sponsored hobby show.

Flood waters invade the Pennsylvania Railroad's Harrisburg passenger station on a drizzly, drab day in March 1936, halting through rail service. For several days the only trains that moved were those that shuttled passengers and business vehicles back and forth between the city and the West Shore. Service to the outside world was slowly resumed as washed-out tracks and flooded terminals were repaired and restored to service.

Over a long period of years special religious services during Easter Week were held daily at noon in the State Education Building. The above picture, taken in 1937, shows crowds leaving the auditorium at the conclusion of a noonday service.

The "front steps" of Harrisburg not only have provided the city with a uniquely beautiful waterfront but also served to protect the bank and park from erosion for more than half a century. The decorative light standards, having become victims of vandalism and flood damage, were removed some years ago.

Twenty-three members of the Harrisburg YMCA boys' club embark on an inspection tour of selected local industries, their transportation being a solid-tire, chain-driven motor truck. The date: 1930.

No booze, drugs, or smoking here! Yet youth had its fill of pleasure at the "Coed Saturday Nighter" programs, sponsored by the local YMCA in the 1940s. Dancing, bowling, table tennis, and just sitting around chatting over a "coke" or chocolate milk served to bring the girls and boys together for a couple hours of fun. Note the absence of blue jeans, sloppy sweat shirts, and worn, dirty sneakers.

The late Jacob Bowers, Pennsylvania Railroad electrical foreman at Harrisburg for many years, was demonstrating a new means of communication between locomotive and engine crews when this photo was taken for publicity purposes by the railroad.

A development of the Westinghouse Electric Company, the train phone was in use on the main lines of the Pennsylvania west of Harrisburg until supplanted by shortwave radio a number of years ago.

In February 1927 local citizens were shocked by the murder of twenty-four-year-old Verna Klink, whose body was dumped into the Susquehanna. Here volunteers search for Verna's body south of the Market Street Bridge, breaking ice in the process.

The accused slayer, Harry Bowman, was defended by an old schoolmate, Solomon Hurwitz (his first case), but was found guilty and sentenced to a life in prison.

Water from Paxton Creek inundated North Cameron Street for its entire length during the Great Flood of March 1936. A used car lot with its collection of submerged vehicles shares the excessive moisture with buildings on the opposite side of the street. Photo taken from the State Street Memorial Bridge.

Gasoline was eighteen and twenty-one cents per gallon and the pumps were operated by hand cranks in 1930 when this photo was taken. Location: southeast corner, Front and Market streets. The coupe sitting at the curbside "Koolmotor" pump belonged to Warren Harder, who took the photo to add to his growing collection of Harrisburg scenes, many of which are reproduced in this book.

The service station, established in 1922, was taken over later by the Cities Service Oil Company, and was managed by Boyd B. Harrington at the time the photo was taken.

It was 1932 and Harrisburg's skyline was changing again. The Bell Telephone and Payne-Shoemaker buildings now hid the majesty of the State Capitol. The Harrisburger Hotel towered over the Penn-Harris, but Front Street retained its residential appearance. George Reist's boat houses were parked in dry dock on City Island and trolleys still rumbled across the Walnut Street Bridge.

The William Penn Museum was still a dream in the minds of Capitol Hill planners in 1938 when a group of visitors from out of town arrived to visit the former museum. The State Library, which formerly shared the building, had already been removed to its new location in the Education Building on Walnut Street at Commonwealth Avenue.

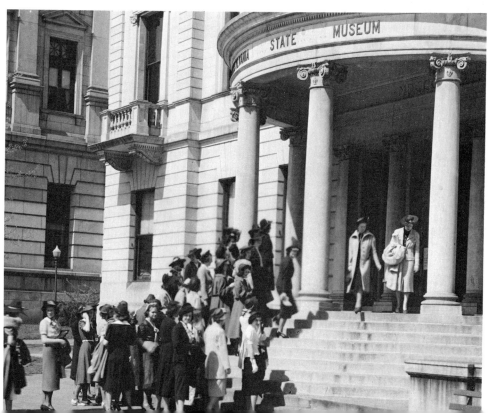

After being shuttled from building to building in a vain search for more space, Pennsylvania's annual Farm Show finally moved into its own spacious new quarters at Cameron and Maclay streets. Again there is talk of moving it, this time to a site outside of the city limits. In the meantime much of the early landscaping shown in this 1938 photo has been removed to provide more parking and loading space.

From Indian paths to modern highways Harrisburg has been a junction point, as this 1941 photo emphasizes. Traffic was still two-way on Front Street, and Dauphin County's new court house was just beginning to take form. Note the shadow of the photographer cast on the sidewalk by a late afternoon sun.

The magic of light on new-fallen snow creates a fairyland scene of mundane surroundings in this night view of Pennsylvania's State House. Towering majestically over all is the brightly illuminated Capitol dome, accentuated by the tracery of bare trees boughs against a winter's night sky.

The Commonwealth's master plan for its Capitol complex gradually takes form with the passing years. This 1944 aerial photograph shows peripheral buildings bordering Walnut and North Streets which were in service at that time. The temporary offices at the rear of the main Capitol building were still in existence at the time the photo was taken.

"Old Shaky," the Walnut Street Bridge, which has survived the vicissitudes of more than eight decades, is getting a new floor in this 1934 photo from Highway Department files. Note the one-way traffic for autos and trolleys alike and workmen risking a tumble into the water far below.

You could still go sledding on city streets in 1941. The boys in this photograph are enjoying a winter's night sport on the grade leading from Forster Street north on Capital in front of the Liquor Control Board Building. No traffic to worry about.

The last trolley to Penbrook had long since made its final run to Harrisburg when removal of the rails was begun in 1940. Workmen here are burning off the top and web of the rails in preparation for a paving project while traffic eases slowly by.

This pretty miss, whose identity remains anonymous, displays the state auto tags for 1930 in a publicity release to the newspapers. Note the single letter and two-digit number which identify special issue tags.

Advertising posters in the windows of Thomas Motor Company showroom, 1002 North Third Street, proclaimed the 1931 model "Willys Six" to be "free wheeling" and the "fastest, most powerful car at its price." The automobile was now well on its way to becoming the dominant means of transportation in our nation.

Harrisburg's extensive park system includes Italian Lake in the uptown area. The lake provides recreation in the form of fishing in the summer and ice skating during the winter months. It has been a popular gathering place for residents ever since 1939, when this picture was taken.

Electrification of the Pennsylvania Railroad between Philadelphia and Harrisburg came about in 1937. Since that time both freight and passenger trains east of the city have been pulled by electric locomotives. Above, a westbound freight train, pulled by a Class P-5 electric engine, has arrived at Enola on a fall day in 1945. Officials who rode the train on an inspection trip and are posing for a photographer are Wayne Shunk, safety supervisor, and Michael Mausteller, assistant freight trainmaster.

Forty years ago a trolley ride to Rockville meant a pleasant trip through rural surroundings north of the city. Pictured here is a Harrisburg Railways car traversing private right-of-way north of the old Linglestown Road. It was the summer of 1936 and street car service had only one more year to go before buses took over this run.

It is January 22, 1938 and a chilly winter air buffets passengers boarding a Third Street trolley at Third and Market streets. The riders are oblivious to the fact that they will probably be riding a street car for the last time. The last day for trolley operation on this route is at hand as bus substitutions continue apace.

216

John Porter, of Dauphin, was a big man. Six feet, three inches tall and tipping the scales at 560 pounds, he towers over his friend John Malehorn in this photo. A professional fat man, he traveled with carnivals for eighteen years before his death at fifty-four, resulting from a heart attack. According to James Megonnell, Sr., Dauphin R.D., who knew him, Porter had "a heart as big as his body." "He was generous to a fault," said Megonnell, "and lived in a home along Stony Creek when not on the road. When he died in 1946 a special coffin had to be built to accommodate his huge body."

On January 23, 1938, a spanking new Harrisburg Railways Company bus pulls up to the curb at Third and Market streets to pick up passengers heading uptown.

The cornerstone of the North Office Building of the Capitol complex is in place and Lieutenant Governor Arthur H. James wields a trowel as ex-Governor Gifford Pinchot (hands in vest pockets), Governor John S. Fisher (looking towards camera), and Secretary of Highways James L. Stuart (back to crowd) look on. The date is July 6, 1928. Note the ladies' hats and men's straw "skimmers" among the crowd watching. Also the trolley signals on the pole nearby.

A steady rain was adding insult to injury on that miserable day in March of 1936 when a local news photographer, safely ensconced on the Mulberry Street Bridge, snapped the watery scene at the lower end of the Pennsylvania Railroad passenger station here. A small cloud of steam indicates an engine working nearby.

A fine old Front Street home makes way for "progress." The former Henry Schuddemage residence at Front and Peffer streets is reduced to a pile of rubble to make way for commercialism of a once prominent residential neighborhood.

Mr. Schuddemage was a building contractor and the city's first building inspector. During log rafting days the Schuddemage family operated a lumber mill along the river.

Cross-river traffic was increasing at a rapid pace in 1926 and plans had been completed for the erection of a larger bridge at Market Street. A Highway Department photographer set up his camera on the east bank to picture progress of work on the heavier piers for the new span between Front and Market and City Island.

Index

(Page numbers in bold face type refer to illustration.)